**Short Studies
from the
Walter Chapin Simpson Center
for the Humanities**

The Center for the Humanities at the University
of Washington was established in 1987 with a
mandate to encourage interdisciplinary activities
in the humanities. Supported by the University
Initiative Fund and endowed in 1997 in the
name of Walter Chapin Simpson, the Center is
dedicated to fostering innovative teaching and
research in the humanities, and to stimulating
exchange and debate on cultural and educational issues, both on and off the University of
Washington campus. Its broader goal is to knit
the academic and civic communities through
a shared fostering of education and culture.
The Simpson Center sponsors a wide range of
activities, including interdisciplinary courses and
collaborative research groups, public lectures,
symposia, arts events, publications, and a
fellowship program for University of Washington
faculty and students.

A Manifesto for Literary Studies

Marjorie Garber

Walter Chapin Simpson Center for the Humanities I University of Washington, Seattle

Copyright © 2003 by the Walter Chapin Simpson Center for the Humanities

Library of Congress Cataloging-in-Publication Data
Garber, Marjorie B.
  A manifesto for literary studies / Marjorie Garber.
     p.   cm.—(Short studies from the Walter Chapin Simpson Center for the Humanities)
  Includes bibliographical references.
  ISBN 0-295-98344-2 (alk. paper)
     1. English literature—History and criticism—Theory, etc.   2. American literature—History and
criticism—Theory, etc.   3. Literature—History and criticism—Theory, etc.   I. Title.   II. Series.
PR21.G36   2003   820.9—dc22   2003062196

Excerpt from "Burnt Norton" in *Four Quartets,* by T. S. Eliot, copyright 1936 by Harcourt, Inc., and renewed
1964 by T. S. Eliot. Reprinted by permission of the publisher.

"The Coming of Wisdom with Time," by William Butler Yeats, from *The Collected Works of W. B. Yeats,
Volume 1: The Poems, Revised,* edited by Richard J. Finneran (New York: Scribner, 1997). Reprinted with
the permission of Scribner, an imprint of Simon & Schuster Adult Publishing Group.

Printed in the United States of America
Distributed by the University of Washington Press
PO Box 50096
Seattle, Washington 98145–5096

www.washington.edu/uwpress

Series Editor
Kathleen Woodward

Series Designer
Christopher Ozubko

Contents

A
Manifesto
for
Literary
Studies

Asking Literary Questions

The title of this volume risks being regarded as vieux jeu *on the one hand, and aggrandizing on the other. Why does something as staid as "literary studies" need a manifesto? And why mobilize that quintessentially political form of the last century, the ardent advocacy of the manifesto, in support of a discipline well established within the academy?*

The fortunes of literary studies have gone up and down during the twentieth and twenty-first centuries with the same volatility as the stock market. And like the stock market, the market in literary studies can be charted with confidence only with the benefit of hindsight.

English studies held the comfortable middle ground of the humanities in U.S. and Anglophile/Anglophone universities through the middle part of the twentieth century. The combined heritage of belletrism and the "little magazines" imparted a certain gloss of creativity and artiness to the practice of reading and writing about poems, novels, plays, and what was then often described as "intellectual prose"—works like Robert Burton's *Anatomy of Melancholy,* for example, or Samuel Johnson's *Lives of the Poets.* Practices like textual explication, often cognate with, or imported from, the study of religious texts, were partnered with literary history, thematic criticism, and the study of images, tropes, and what was called literary influence—the indebtedness and echoes of one literary work to another—whether such influence was deemed serene or "anxious." *Intertextuality,* a term borrowed from French, offered an adjustment to the question of influence by seeing it as a two-way street, and also by emphasizing the agency of the text over that of the controlling "author." Texts could converse with one another whether or not the author was consciously speaking—or listening. The conscious/unconscious borderline was a natural topic for scholars steeped in the heritage of romanticism, whether or not they acknowledged the pervasive influence of Sigmund Freud's writings on the development of twentieth-century art and culture.

An infusion of exciting and provocative theoretical writing, again largely continental in origin, coming to the United States from France, Germany, and the U.K., made "literary studies"—or, more properly then, "literary theory"—the star, and also in some views the bad child, of humanistic work in the 1970s and 1980s. Intellectual practices such as semiotics, phenomenology, and structuralism changed the way critics and scholars read literature, and "literature" itself changed with the onset of lively debates about the literary canon, cultural inclusiveness, and popular culture. Whether described under the heading of *poststructuralism, deconstruction,* or *postmodernity,* the work of European writers like Roland Barthes, Pierre Bourdieu,

Raymond Williams, Jacques Derrida, Jacques Lacan, and Michel Foucault shifted attention to issues of text and agency.

A phrase like "the linguistic turn" (later transformed into "the cultural turn") signaled a high-water mark for the prestige of this particular mode of literariness in the late twentieth century. As Lynn Hunt and Victoria Bonnell note in their introduction to *Beyond the Cultural Turn* (1999), the publication of two key works in 1973—Hayden White's *Metahistory: The Historical Imagination in Nineteenth-Century Europe* and Clifford Geertz's *The Interpretation of Cultures: Selected Essays*—established the importance of techniques derived from literary studies for the disciplines of history and cultural anthropology.[1] White's book uses terms like *trope* and *emplotment* to argue for a deep structure of thought that organized historical research at the linguistic level, working with categories derived from the literary scholars Kenneth Burke and Northrop Frye. Geertz's idea of a "thick description" of cultures presented symbols, artifacts, social arrangements, and rituals as "texts" that could be read as a consistent story, or "interpretation"—a word itself grounded in literary study. The powerful influence of Geertz has naturalized the phrase "interpretation of cultures" so that it no longer offers any hint of the jostling of disciplines.[2]

White introduced his study with a strong claim about the relationship of history to language that established the first as dependent upon the second: "In this theory I treat the historical work as what it most manifestly is: a verbal structure in the form of a narrative prose discourse." Histories, he maintained, "contain a deep structural content which is generally poetic, and specifically linguistic, in nature, and which serves as the precritically accepted paradigm of what a distinctively 'historical' explanation should be."[3] His table of contents was explicitly indebted to Frye's structuralist account of genre, with chapters such as "Michelet: Historical Realism as Romance," "Ranke: Historical Realism as Comedy," "Tocqueville: Historical Realism as Tragedy," and "Burckhardt: Historical Realism as Satire."

"The culture of a people is an ensemble of texts," wrote Geertz in his celebrated essay on the Balinese cockfight:

> Such an extension of the notion of a text beyond written material, and
> even beyond verbal, is, though metaphorical, not of course, all that novel.

The *interpretatio naturae* tradition of the middle ages, which, culminating in Spinoza, attempted to read nature as Scripture, the Nietszchean effort to treat value systems as glosses on the will to power (or the Marxian one to treat them as glosses on property relations), and the Freudian replacement of the enigmatic text of the manifest dream with the plain one of the latent, all offer precedents, if not equally recommendable ones. But the idea remains theoretically undeveloped; and the more profound corollary, so far as anthropology is concerned, that cultural forms can be treated as texts, as imaginative works built out of social materials, has yet to be systematically exploited.[4]

"A deep structural content which is *generally poetic, and specifically linguistic*"; "An *extension of the notion of the text* beyond written material, and even beyond verbal." Both White and Geertz found the models of linguistic and literary analysis instrumental and clarifying as they grappled with fresh ways of understanding the methodologies of their own disciplines. Indeed, as such passages from their work make evident, these scholars would come to argue that history and anthropology were, in a way, modes of reading and writing. "As in more familiar exercises in close reading," Geertz writes in his concluding paragraph to the cockfight essay, "one can start anywhere in a culture's repertoire of forms and end up anywhere else." In later writings, he would sum this up in the phrase "the Text analogy," which, when linked with "interpretive theory," allows for new reconfigurations of social thought.[5]

The idea of a "master discourse" has long fallen into disuse and even into disrepute, but if there is any discourse that holds the mastery in these excerpts from two groundbreaking works of cultural theory it is *literary studies*. How quickly we forget.

In the years that followed these brilliant appropriations *from literary studies,* the appropriators were themselves re-appropriated *by literary critics* and established in the rhetorical position of mastery. New historicists Steven Mullaney and Stephen Greenblatt both invoke Geertz's methodology: "Employing a kind of 'thick description' in Clifford Geertz's sense of the phrase," Mullaney writes, "I examine diverse sources and events, cultural as well as literary, in an effort to situate the popular stage within the larger symbolic economy of Elizabethan and Jacobean England."[6] Greenblatt cites a passage from Geertz comparing Elizabethan and Majapahit royal progresses at a key turning point in his own essay on Shakespeare's *Henry IV* plays.[7]

Literary critic J. Hillis Miller, a specialist in the British nineteenth-century novel, lists White as an important figure in the development of modern theories of narrative. "The inclusion of Hayden White," he writes, "is testimony to the fact that in recent years history writing as well as fictional narratives have been addressed by narrative theorists."[8]

Authority in literary critical—and literary theorical—writings began, increasingly, to derive from such voices. Not only White and Geertz, but anthropologist Mary Douglas *(Purity and Danger),* sociologist Pierre Bourdieu, cultural historian Robert Darnton, and others were cited in argument and epigraph, and a new vocabulary became the common medium of exchange: "*Culture, practice, relativism, truth, discourse, narrative, microhistory,* and various other terms," note Hunt and Bonnell, were in general use across many of the social science disciplines.[9] But these same terms became words to conjure with in literary studies as well, together with others that also originated in social-scientific or scientific disciplines: *genealogy, archaeology, agency, paradigm.*

Not long after their eager engagement with "the linguistic turn," historians and others drew back, themselves returning to an emphasis on empirical data, sometimes in conjunction with theoretical arguments, and sometimes to trump them. In a book pointedly called *Telling the Truth about History,* Joyce Appleby, Lynn Hunt, and Margaret Jacob noted the difficulties of aligning postmodern theory with historical practice:

> If postmodern cultural anthropology is any guide, the concern with developing causal explanations and social theories would be replaced in a post-modernist history with a focus on self-reflexivity and on problems of literary construction: how does the historian as author construct his or her text, how is the illusion of authenticity produced, what creates a sense of truthfulness to the facts and a warranty of closeness to past reality (or the "truth-effect" as it is sometimes called)? The implication is that the historian does not in fact capture the past in faithful fashion but rather, like the novelist, gives the appearance of doing so.[10]

The authors were at pains to say that they did not reject all the ideas of postmodernist thinkers, noting that the text analogy and various cultural and linguistic approaches had helped to disengage historians from models such as Marxism and other economic and social determinisms, while also "puncturing the shield of science behind which reductionism often hid." But "linguistic determinism" also presents a problem, they argued. And since postmodernism "throws into question the modern narrative form," key methodologies for writing history, including historiography, narrative, and storytelling, were all subject to critique. Yet historians have to tell stories, they claimed, in order to make sense of the past, as well as to reach toward practical political solutions for the future. So these authors, all historians, suggested that there was a point at which members of the historical profession, however initially energized by the likes of Derrida and Foucault, had to part company with them, to rejoin the referent and leave the play of the signifier, or to leave the "text" and rejoin the "world." In fact, Appleby, Hunt, and Jacob wrote in 1994, "a similar kind of crisis that foreshadows a turning away from the postmodern view can be seen in almost every field of knowledge or learning today."[11]

A few key observations might be made about these ideas:

- They tie "the linguistic turn" (quickly broadened, to accommodate anthropology, into "the cultural turn") to postmodern theory, thus eliding the linguistic, the literary, the cultural-anthropological, and the philosophical.

- They ultimately set aside postmodernism as antifoundationalist and thus likely to pose questions rather than seek solutions. ("In place of plot and character, history and individuality, perhaps even meaning itself, the most thoroughgoing postmodernists would offer an 'interminable pattern without meaning,' a form of writing closer to modern music and certain postmodern novels."[12])

- They generalize a "crisis"—supplementary to the fabled "crisis in the humanities"—that led, or would lead, or was then currently leading participants "in almost every field of knowledge or learning" to turn away from the postmodern view, and thus from the temporary hegemony of humanistic and literary critical studies.

The return of the "empirical" after the heady attractions of the ungrounded "theoretical" had its effects upon literary scholars as well as upon historians, anthropologists, and sociologists. Inevitably, perhaps, chroniclers began to contemplate "the historic turn." The editor of a volume on *The Historic Turn in the Human Sciences* noted that there had been a proliferation of historical emphases across the disciplines: "the 'new historicism' in literary and legal theory, a revived interest in 'history in philosophy,' a historically oriented 'new institutionalism' and other historical approaches in political science and economics, 'ethnohistory' in anthropology," and so on.[13] Literary critic Steven Mullaney offered in his contribution to the volume a view of the place of literary study that conveyed a sharp difference from where it might have been presumed to be in the 1970s and 1980s:

> The literary is thus conceived neither as a separate and separable aesthetic realm nor as a mere product of culture—a reflection of ideas and ideologies produced elsewhere—but as one realm among many for the negotiation and production of social meaning, of historical subjects, and of the systems of power that at once enable and constrain those subjects.[14]

Manifest in this compact assertion was a suspicion of, and a demotion of, the "separable aesthetic" and the "mere product of culture"; the profession of literature and the texts that were its objects were to be players in social change. Where the *Telling the Truth* historians had reflected on the potential disappearance of "meaning itself" under the lens of the kind of postmodern theory that had once, and recently, dominated literary study, Mullaney, a new-historicist critic of the early-modern period, declared literary study's newly rediscovered investment in "the negotiation and production of social meaning."

"The literary" had changed, and changed substantially, at least in historicist eyes. "The literary" in this avatar also considered itself "one realm among many," not in any privileged place of influence or taste-making. As the century drew to a close, the question of literary study's place in the intellectual and academic hierarchy was an unsettled matter. Even literally. Suddenly the word "material" was everywhere (to be contrasted, presumably, with its antonym "formal," but also with the complicatedly intellectual and highly verbal playing fields of theory). "Material culture" and "the material book" were phrases to conjure with, as book series on "art and material culture," "design and material culture," "American material culture and folklore," and "gender and material culture" proliferated. Books on *The Body as Material Culture, Children and Material Culture, Chimpanzee Material Culture,* and *Cognition and Material Culture* crowded the bookshops—and these titles are only the briefest of selections from the Bs and Cs. Literary critics, once to be styled by preference "literary theorists," were now, increasingly, scholars of material culture.

Furthermore, the rise of cultural studies and other interdisciplinary approaches to social and cultural practice caught the eye, and the disapproving glance, of many former, retired, or disgruntled academics, some now transformed into journalists or government officials, who unilaterally declared a "culture war." Deconstruction, a reading practice akin to American New Criticism, was parodied as a plot of the Left. When deconstructive critic Paul de Man was discovered to have had a complicated past involving possible collaboration with the Germans during World War II, deconstruction also became a "fascist" plot. Race-class-and-gender, or race-class-gender-and-sexuality, were deemed unworthy "political" objects of humanistic attention, and attention to "colonialism" (even for a discipline like English studies, which emerged as a university subject at the height of the British Empire) was likewise dismissed as irrelevant political meddling by scholars who would be better off restricting their activities to the library, the archive, the museum—and the (undergraduate) classroom. What was most disturbing about these attacks was their mean-spiritedness and the shoddiness of the "research" that produced them, often consisting of sitting in on a single class by a given professor, or listing and belittling the titles of courses or of conference papers, many never read in their entirety by the journalists who mocked them. But there is no doubt that this strategy was effective, and doubly so, since those attacked began to attack back, providing precisely the kind of partisan evidence their critics had wished into being.

I am conscious here of reporting old news and chronicling old battles to which I myself have no desire to return; few who lived through this period would welcome a resumption of hostilities, which now seem both fevered and distant. But I mention those developments for a reason: to point out that the scholars singled out for particular opprobrium in books of the late 1980s and early 1990s were, almost all of them, professors of literary studies. Roger Kimball's grumpy but highly successful diatribe, *Tenured Radicals,* begins in the spirit of a manifesto: "It is no secret that the academic study of the humanities in this country is in a state of crisis."[15] He then goes on, in the second paragraph of his book, to name some of the principal culprits: "Princeton University's Elaine Showalter" (gender), "University of Pennsylvania's Houston Baker" (race), and "Duke University's Fredric Jameson" (Marxist politics). All three are professors of literature. Other humanistic disciplines also sustained periodic swipes, especially those that led to a concern with politics or popular culture (as in the work of philosophers Richard Rorty and Stanley Cavell). But the "academics" the critics loved to hate were more often than not those trained as literary critics.

As I have noted, this strategy was successful. Not only did the country take notice that the sky was falling, so too did the critics and scholars mentioned. Even those scholars watching the debates from the sidelines (not the "margins," which were now at the center) began to feel the pressure. Once a suspicion is planted, it is very difficult indeed to uproot it; "tenured radicals," spiffy phrase that it was, had changed the way the academy regarded itself. Like the insinuations of Iago ("taken together with the other proofs") these proofs of nothing multiplied to produce a firm conviction that something had gone wrong. And, partially as a result, the place of literary studies in the pantheon of the humanities came under both tacit and explicit critiques. Younger—and older—scholars of literature shifted their interests, whether consciously or (more likely) unconsciously, away from the play of language, the ambivalent ambiguities of the signifier, and the modes of counterintuitive argument that had marked the most brilliant literary work of the 1970s and 1980s (and, indeed, the 1940s and the 1950s), toward less controversial terrain and more supposedly objective (and even "scientific") methodologies like history, the "sociology of knowledge," and cognitive theory. Literary study was in the process of disowning itself.

Genteelly, professionally, persuasively, and without an apparent consciousness of what might be lost in the process, departments of literature and literary study have shifted their emphasis. This return to history is in fact a return, not a leap or an evasion. Trends in intellectual work tend to be cyclical, with attention shifting from text to context, from author or artist to historical-cultural surround, from theory to practice, and from micro- to macro-analysis (in literary study, close reading vs. meta-narratives). A great deal of the most recent work in literary studies is deeply informative, much of it represents what used to be called "a contribution to knowledge," and almost all of it is professionally honed, if not glossy. If little is provocative, perhaps that is to be expected after a couple of decades of high-profile contestation. There are many ways of doing inventive scholarship, and painstaking literary-historical work, like the kind of literary work that admires and imitates the scientism of cognitive theory, can at its best also be imaginatively interesting.

Some literary historians and historicist critics within departments of literary study are in danger of forgetting, or devaluing, the history of their own craft and practice, which is based not only on the contextual understanding of literary works but also on the words on the page. Counterintuitive interpretation, reading that understands the adjacency of literature, fantasy, and dream, the subliminal association of words through patterns of sound or tics of meaning, the serendipity of images and ideas, the sometimes unintended echoes of other writers, the powerful formal scaffolding of rhetoric or of genre—all these are as richly transgressive as any political interpreter might desire, and as elusively evocative as any archive-trained researcher could wish to unearth or detect.

The specific contribution of literary studies to intellectual life inheres in the way it *differs from* other disciplines—in its methodology and in its aim—rather than in the way it *resembles* them. What literary scholars can offer to the readers of all texts (not just those explicitly certified as "literature") is a way of *asking literary questions:* questions about the *way* something means, rather than *what* it means, or even *why*. It is not that literary studies is uninterested in the what and the why—indeed, in recent years such questions have preoccupied scholars whose models are drawn from adjacent disciplines like history and social science. But literariness, which lies at the heart of literary studies, is a matter of style, form, genre, and verbal interplay, as well as of social and political context—not only the realm of reference and context but also intrinsic structural elements like grammar, rhetoric, and syntax; tropes and figures; assonance and echo. A manifesto for literary studies will claim an unapologetic freestanding power to change the world by reading: by reading what is manifest, and what is latent, within and through the language of the text.

The present volume, appropriately published in booklet form like many manifestos of the past, is an attempt to remind us of the specificity of what it means to ask literary questions, and the pleasure of thinking through and with literature. It is a manifesto in the sense that it invites strong declarations and big ideas, rather than impeccable small contributions to edifices long under construction. And it is also, in the old and honorable sense used by Sidney and by Shelley, a defense of poetry, or an apology for poetry. The best way for literary scholars to reinstate the study of literature, language, and culture as a key player among the academic humanities is to do what we do best, to engage in big public questions of intellectual importance and to address them by using the tools of our trade, which include not only material culture but also theory, interpretation, linguistic analysis, and a close and passionate attention to the rich allusiveness, deep ambivalence, and powerful slipperiness that is language in action. The future importance of literary studies—and, if we care about such things, its intellectual and cultural prestige both among the other disciplines and in the world—will come from taking risks, and not from playing it safe.

1   Victoria E. Bonnell and Lynn Hunt, eds., *Beyond the Cultural Turn* (Berkeley: University of California Press, 1999), 2.

2   Hayden White, *Metahistory: The Historical Imagination in Nineteenth-Century Europe* (Baltimore and London: The Johns Hopkins University Press, 1973), ix.

3   Ibid.

4   Clifford Geertz, *The Interpretation of Cultures* (New York: Basic Books, 1973), 452, 448–49.

5   Clifford Geertz, "Blurred Genres: The Reconfiguration of Social Thought," in *Local Knowledge: Further Essays in Interpretive Anthropology* (New York: Basic Books, 1983), 30.

6   Steven Mullaney, *The Place of the Stage: License, Play, and Power in Renaissance England* (Chicago and London: University of Chicago Press, 1988), x.

7   Stephen Greenblatt, "Invisible Bullets," in *Shakespearean Negotiations: The Circulation of Social Energy in Renaissance England* (Berkeley and Los Angeles: University of California Press, 1988), 65.

8   J. Hillis Miller, "Narrative," in *Critical Terms for Literary Study*, 2d ed., ed. Frank Lentricchia and Thomas McLaughlin (Chicago and London: University of Chicago Press, 1995), 69.

9   Bonnell and Hunt, eds., *Beyond the Cultural Turn*, 25. Italics in original.

10   Joyce Appleby, Lynn Hunt, and Margaret Jacob, *Telling the Truth about History* (New York and London: W. W. Norton, 1994), 231.

11   Ibid., 231–36.

12   Ibid., 232–33, quoting Elizabeth Deeds Ermarth, *Sequel to History: Postmodernism and the Crisis of Representational Time* (Princeton: Princeton University Press, 1992), 212.

13   Terence J. McDonald, ed., *The Historic Turn in the Human Sciences* (Ann Arbor: University of Michigan Press, 1996), 1.

14   Steven Mullaney, "Discursive Forums, Cultural Practices: History and Anthropology in Literary Study," in *The Historic Turn in the Human Sciences*, ed. McDonald, 163.

15   Roger Kimball, *Tenured Radicals: How Politics Has Corrupted Our Higher Education* (New York: Harper and Row, 1990), xi.

Who Owns "Human Nature"?

The proper study of mankind is man.

ALEXANDER POPE, "ESSAY ON MAN"

I

In the wake of the events of September 11, 2001, people around the world struggled to understand what the terrorist attacks on the World Trade Center and the Pentagon could possibly tell us about "human nature." The London *Guardian* suggested that "we are struggling to adapt our perception of the world, our safety in it, and our understanding of human nature—to incorporate a new dimension of evil."[1] A letter to *Newsday* remarked that the actions taken by rescue workers at the World Trade Center showed that "when it is required of people to disregard basic human nature, which is greed and selfishness, and put the needs of a civilization first, it can be done."[2] (The author of this sober assessment was a high school senior.) The *Los Angeles Times* observed that the job of a firefighter seemed "almost antithetical to human nature: When everyone else flees from danger, they run toward it."[3] And an obituary notice for one of the thousands of victims lost in the World Trade Center attack began with a poignant observation: "It is a quirk of human nature that the person who does an act of kindness may forget it, but the recipient does not."[4] What is "human nature"? And what kind of measure can define and assess it?

"It's just human nature," people often say with a shrug about cultural, social, political, and moral actions from greed to optimism to studied indifference. It is human nature to think we can win the lottery; it is human nature not to want to "get involved" in reporting a crime; it is human nature to believe that our current affair of the heart is true love. (Thus Samuel Johnson defined a second marriage as "the triumph of hope over experience.") The shameful silence of the thirty-eight witnesses to the rape and murder of Kitty Genovese on a quiet street in Kew Gardens, New York, in 1964 (none of whom called police until after she was dead) was attributed to human nature, but so is kindness to animals, and a passion for team sports. The "dark side of human nature" turns up in many journalistic accounts of mayhem, trickery, and violence. And it is not just "life," but art, that is periodically called to witness. A production of *The Nutcracker* ballet is said by a critic to plumb the "tragic side of human nature." Reality television is said to cast a "bleakly pessimistic light . . . on human nature."[5]

"Human nature" is praised, or blamed, for the good behavior of samaritans and the bad behavior of politicians. Journalists use it all the time. A reporter writing during the Monica Lewinsky scandal announced that "human nature being what it is" in the case of male politicians and female interns, we have a long way to go before attaining equality between the sexes.[6] The idea that Americans could quickly forget the irregularities of the presidential election "contradicts whatever we might have observed about human nature,"[7] wrote Francine Prose. It was simply "a matter of human nature" that political contributors wanted to go to Senator Hillary Clinton's new house for a fund-raiser, observed Democratic strategist James Carville.[8] The national debate about stem cell research suggested to conservative columnist George Will that "the parties represent different sensibilities—different stances toward nature, including human nature."[9]

What in the world *is* "human nature"? Few phrases are used so confidently and promiscuously, by parents and children, religious figures and laity, optimists and pessimists, humanists and scientists. And few phrases have been responsible for so much disinformation, or so much attitudinizing. John Keats thought it finer than scenery. William Wordsworth exulted that it had been born again in the early years of the French Revolution. Karl Marx called it an "aesthetic delusion."[10] Journalist turned fiction writer Anna Quindlen, disclaiming any right to be considered an ethicist or a philosopher, announced with mock modesty, "I'm a novelist. My work is human nature. Real life is really all I know."[11]

But where thinkers from the sixteenth to the mid-twentieth centuries—from William Shakespeare to David Hume to Virginia Woolf—felt both the necessity and the right to offer opinions on this key phrase and its ramifications, studies of human nature in the latter years have focused, symptomatically, on science: evolutionary biology and psychology, gene theory, behaviorism, and cultural evolution. It is a suggestive fact about human nature that it was once the intellectual property of poets, philosophers, and political theorists and is now largely the domain of scientists.

"Genome Project Can't Explain Human Nature," declared the caption of a *Boston Globe* letter to the editor responding to the mapping of the human genome by two scientific teams. The letter writer, voicing an opinion shared by many commentators after the reports disclosed that humans had fewer genes than formerly believed, observes that it is absurd to expect "that the answers science provides can explain the unique nature of humanity."[12] The news that human beings had only thirty thousand genes, not many more than go into the making of a roundworm, a fruit fly, or a plant, and that only about three hundred of those genes are different from the genome of a mouse, raised what the media persistently called "humbling" questions about how to explain "human complexity" and what it means to be human.[13] And yet this is just what is so ardently desired, at least in some quarters—an answer to the question, an answer that science alone is thought, these days, to provide.

In a book entitled *Our Posthuman Future* (2002), political scientist Francis Fukuyama warns against recent developments in biotechnology—from cloning to Prozac, from plastic surgery to genetic engineering—that threaten to modify human nature. At stake was the view, strongly championed by Fukuyama, that an essential and unchanging theory of human nature is "fundamental to our notions of justice, morality, and the good life," and that tampering with the genome may cause us "to lose our humanity."[14]

Is "human nature" fixed or mutable, something that science helps us to understand, or something that science itself has the capacity to change, something that was once powerfully described by literature and philosophy, but has now become the realm of science? How did "human nature," once deemed the proper study of mankind, get to be the privileged territory of geneticists and biologists?

II

The term *human nature* can be inflected on the first word (*human* nature, as contrasted with that of animals, angels, or God) or the second (human *nature,* what is intrinsic rather than eccentric or acculturated for human beings). The first of these modes suggests a difference *between* humankind and other beings, and thus implicitly asserts the commonality of *human* experience in contrast with that of others. (The paradoxical phrase "the human nature of Christ," common in many works of

Christian theology, points up the issue, as does the section of Jared Diamond's evolutionary study, *The Third Chimpanzee,* that focuses on a quartet of activities he calls "uniquely human": language, art, agriculture, and substance addiction.[15]) That which is particular to humans in this concept of human nature is, ordinarily, what differentiates them from beasts or gods. In Western thought this has been associated with the so-called "Great Chain of Being," derived from Hellenic philosophy and adapted for Christian and neo-Platonic use in the medieval and early modern periods. The *ur*-text here may be the eighth Psalm, "What is man, that thou art mindful of him? And the son of man, that thou visitest him? For thou hast made him a little lower than the angels" (Ps. 8:4–5), or its passionate adaptation in Hamlet's famous speech of existential despair:

> What a piece of work is a man! How noble in reason! How infinite in faculty! In form and moving how express and admirable, in action, how like an angel, in apprehension, how like a god;. . . . And yet, to me, what is this quintessence of dust? (*Hamlet* 2.2.303–08)[16]

If we change the inflection to stress the second term rather than the first (human *nature*), we alter the field of interpretation considerably, since what is now emphasized is what could be called a difference *within.* What is "natural" to humans and what is "learned," "cultural," "adapted," or even "unnatural"? Both of these emphases are operative in the history of the phrase, and both have had telling effects on how the various disciplines of the humanities have understood their relation to the age-old question, "What is man?" Yet in fact it is a question not frequently posed, these days, within the humanities. This is the conundrum that has provoked my inquiry.

Humanists have, by and large, abandoned their claims to an interest in this most interesting of problems, tending in recent years to regard the phrase *human nature* as a reductive mode of fuzzy thinking. This skepticism is frequently justified, for all too often human nature turns up (on student papers, for example, or in journalistic opinion pieces) as an *answer,* a solution or explanation for a quirk or a kink of character. If the explanation for human action, or human behavior, whether in literature or in life, is simply "human nature," then analysis and interpretation have been replaced by tautology. In addition, for twentieth- and twenty-first-century humanists the word *human* itself often seems like a version of what has been called "essentializing"—that is, a refusal to acknowledge both cultural difference and the formative influence of history, economics, regionalism, personal biography, and other social and political elements that go into the "construction" of a person in the world. Feminists and other cultural theorists have also called into question the troublesome word *man,* which seemed to some to erase *woman* in a gesture toward the universal subject. Before we conclude that this gesture is a peculiarity of ideologues and latter-day separatists, we might recall that Hamlet parses the word in a similar fashion at the end of that same famous speech—a speech that, though often misremembered as a soliloquy, is in fact addressed to his mischievous schoolfellows, Rosencrantz and Guildenstern. "Man delights not me—nor woman neither, though by your smiling you seem to say so," he tells them, making the artful shift (no one does this better than Shakespeare) from the general to the particular, and thus exposing the intrinsic ambiguities and doubleness implicit in the grandest of ideas (*Hamlet* 2.2.309–10). Is *man* a term that transcends mere gender, or is it a name that produces gender trouble? In any case, *man* has fallen out of favor in literary and cultural studies, together with universal pronouns like *we* and *us,* leaving the field of "human nature" open to other disciplines. Thus Clifford Geertz could refer parenthetically, in 1973, to "(what used, in a simpler day, to be called 'human nature')."[17]

But this shift in the disciplinary custody of "human nature" has serious consequences for the value of that amorphous enterprise called "the humanities." For if the place to investigate "human nature" is not "the humanities," what is the use of the humanistic disciplines? What else gives them cultural authority? And, equally to the point, what is the use of funding, supporting, studying, and teaching them?

"Human nature" is an artifact of culture and language, of fantasy and projection. In other words, the very idea of human nature as a normative, identifiable essence is both a political and a psychological wish, with important side effects. What is most fascinating to me about the concept of human nature is the way the quest for it has become a self-fulfilling dream, a lure of full self-knowledge, a ruse of research paradigms and protocols from the theological to the anthropological, from behaviorism to genomics. During the Enlightenment it was political philosophers; during the nineteenth century it was religious believers, psychologists, and anthropologists; today it is scientists working at the level of the gene.

III

The migration of "human nature" across disciplines in the last several hundred years, from moral philosophy to religion, psychology, Freud and Freudianism, and the new Darwinists, is a fascinating history, represented in literally hundreds of works such as *Human Nature and Railroads* (1915); *Human Nature in Business* (1920); *Human Nature and Management* (1929); *Human Nature and Christian Marriage* (1958); *Human Nature in Politics* (1977); *Human Nature and Predictability* (1981); *Human Nature at the Millennium* (1997) and so on. Starting as early as Thomas Boston's resoundingly titled *Human Nature in Its Fourfold State of Primitive Integrity, Entire Depravity, Begun Recovery and Consummate Happiness or Misery* (1729), phrases like "human nature and . . . " or "human nature in . . . " or "the human nature of . . . " became the watchwords of a certain kind of cultural advice, analysis, and wisdom. "Suffering," "the gospel," "the nature of evil," "the peace problem," "world disorder," and "selling goods"— all have been linked with "human nature" in the titles of books in the last century. The books on business and management, and indeed some of the books on Christianity, are boosterist in spirit: "America," as well as "Christianity," seems to be a consequence of, or a fulfillment of, the best in "human nature."

Eighteenth-century political theorists like David Hume had speculated on the nature of "human nature" in quest of a theory of the individual, of reason, and of human agency. But later accounts by thinkers from Sigmund Freud to Charles Darwin radically altered the question of control and mastery. Who or what controlled "human nature"? Was man indeed a rational animal, or rather a creature dominated by the unconscious or by heredity and evolution? Karl Marx's skepticism about the development of human nature as an ideology by political theorists is still a cogent argument today: "The prophets of the eighteenth century," Marx contended, "saw this individual not as an historical result, but as the starting-point of history; not as something evolving in the course of history, but posited by nature, because for them this individual was in conformity with nature, in keeping with their idea of human nature. This delusion has been characteristic of every new epoch hitherto."[18] Whether delusory or not, the relationship of the individual to human nature came to dominate a whole range of social, cultural, political, and religious writings concerned with human betterment.

In some cases medical science seemed to offer specific answers, as if human nature were a pathological symptom. It was the nerves, or the glands, that held the key, in scientific studies like *The Mysteries of Human Nature Explained by a New System of Nervous Physiology* (1857), by J. Stanley Grimes, a professor of medical jurisprudence, or *The Glands Regulating Personality: A Study of the Glands of Internal Secretion in Relation to the Types of Human Nature* (1921) by Louis Berman, a doctor of medicine.[19] "The future," thought Berman, "belongs to the biochemist" since the glands are really in charge: "In short, they control human nature, and whoever controls them, controls human nature." Thus "the answer to the question 'What is Man?' is 'Man is regulated by his Glands of Internal Secretion.'" The upshot was a theory of glandular social betterment: "The raising of the general level of intelligence by the judicious use of endocrine extracts will mean a good deal to the sincere statesmen" and may thus help to prevent war.[20]

This focus on the operation of a particular internal body part, the glandular system, to explain everything about human nature, runs counter to the lofty and seemingly timeless generalizations of philosophy. But the borderline between the timeless and the local or situational is constantly being crossed. A good example is offered by the surprising itinerary of John Dewey's *Human Nature and Conduct,* an influential work of social psychology written in 1918, at the end of World War I, and published in 1922. Addressing issues such as "habit" and the "alterability of human nature," Dewey, a philosopher and educational reformer, pointed out that modern warfare operates on quite a different basis from that of the *Iliad,* the "classic expression of war's traditional psychology as well as the source of the literary tradition regarding its motives and glories." Idealized figures like Helen, Hector, and Achilles were long gone, he noted. "The activities that evoke and incorporate a war are no longer personal love, love of glory, or the soldier's love of his own privately amassed booty, but are of a collective, prosaic political and economic nature." This, indeed, was the very reason why literature is invoked to glorify the "mass movements of soldiery" deployed by "a depersonalized general staff":

> The more horrible a depersonalized scientific mass war becomes, the more necessary it is to find universal ideal motives to justify it. Love of Helen of Troy has become a burning love for all humanity, and hatred of the foe symbolizes a hatred of all the unrighteousness and injustice and oppression which he embodies. The more prosaic the actual causes, the more necessary it is to find glowingly sublime motives.

"Such considerations," Dewey continues, "destroy that argument for [war's] necessary continuance which is based on the immutability of specified forces in original human nature."[21] He wrote this dark account of the "alterability of human nature" at the end of World War I. But his sentiments would be invoked by the U.S. Government in 1944, when *Human Nature and Conduct* was reprinted by the War Department as *War Department Education Manual EM 618,* "an aid in instruction in certain educational activities of the armed forces."[22] Thus by the end of World War II, John Dewey's ironic and trenchant account of human nature in ancient and modern warfare had become part of the curriculum of the United States Armed Forces Institute setting out a program for the manipulation of public perception. Seldom has the timeless been more directly placed in the service of the times. To a twenty-first-century reader, Dewey's resounding phrases about "depersonalized scientific mass war" and the instrumental rhetoric of "unrighteousness," "injustice," and "oppression" will carry yet another set of local meanings.

As Dewey's reading of Homer will suggest, poetry and literature have not been completely shut out in the gradual move of "human nature" toward the social and the scientific. Following the emergence of the phrase in eighteenth-century philosophy, the romantic poets adopted the term with enthusiasm, and by the beginning of the twentieth century "human nature" had become both ubiquitous and commonplace in literary language, appearing regularly in the writings of belletrists of all kinds. Virginia Woolf—a writer with a distinctly unromantic sensibility—seems to have employed it as a matter of course. Reviewing an edition of Montaigne's *Essays,* Woolf observes that he "never ceases to pour scorn upon the misery, the weakness, the vanity of human nature." She congratulates Defoe for dealing with it ("He belongs . . . to the school of the great plain writers, whose work is founded upon what is most persistent, though not most seductive, in human nature") and suggests that Jane Austen was the doyenne of the field ("Her gaze passes straight to the mark, and we know precisely where, upon the map of human nature, that mark is"). As for George Eliot, "she gathers in her large grasp a great bunch of the main elements of human nature and groups them together with a tolerant and wholesome understanding."[23] To illuminate human nature is, in all of these cases, something to be sought, and praised.

Woolf is a novelist as well as an essayist, and it may be imagined that she found some authorial utility in the concept of human nature as it plays into the business of creating characters and social dramas. But in the works of her contemporary and fellow-essayist T. S. Eliot—a very different kind of writer—the term also surfaces with surprising regularity. Likewise Eliot speaks easily of "that dolorous aspect of human nature which in comedy is best portrayed by Molière" and of William Blake's "capacity for considerable understanding of human nature." By building "an attitude of self-dramatization" into some of his heroes, Eliot thought, Shakespeare was "illustrating, consciously or unconsciously, human nature."[24] Plainly in the 1920s and 1930s, when these pieces were written, "human nature" as a general category was itself alive and well in the minds of major writers of fiction, essays, poetry, and drama. Yet the appearance of the concept today in literary discourse is something of an anomaly and a throwback. The term itself is suspect. In a multicultural world, how could there be *one* "human nature"?

Literary critic Harold Bloom's insistence on Shakespeare as the inventor of "the human," while hardly a new claim for Shakespeare studies, was startling in its assumption of a single "human" point of view, as embodied in Bloom's free-wheeling use of the word *we* to mean *I:* "Can we conceive of ourselves without Shakespeare?" he asks rhetorically. And, "Our ideas as to what makes the self authentically human owe more to Shakespeare than ought to be possible."[25] It is this magisterial and unquestioning *we* that marks the problem for some modern theorists—and makes Bloom's approach so comforting for some readers. This *we* is as important to the book's success as its effusive lionization of Shakespeare—a return to an older fashion of speaking.

What do we mean when we say "we"? or "I"? or, for that matter, "you" or "they"? Who is speaking when I say "I"? What is "the human" in this sense? And how is it counterpoised to more theoretical notions of the "inhuman" and the "posthuman," with technology, as well as with what philosophers in the last century called "the human condition"? Hannah Arendt contrasts "the problem of human nature" with the "conditions of human existence—life itself, natality and mortality, worldliness, plurality, and the earth," which "can never 'explain' what we are or answer the question of who we are for the simple reason that they never condition us absolutely."[26] Jean-François Lyotard asks, "[W]hat if human beings, in humanism's sense, were in the process of, constrained into, becoming inhuman," and "what if what is 'proper' to humankind were to be inhabited by the inhuman?"—a question increasingly asked, as well, by cybertheorists and students of modern technology and communication.[27] Are we "electrical," as is claimed by a book called *The Post-Human Condition?*[28] Or are we in fact relentlessly and deterministically "biological," as has been asserted, with authority, by sociobiologist E. O. Wilson?[29]

IV

I want now to turn directly to an examination of the term *human nature* as it has appeared in the writings of late-twentieth- and twenty-first-century scientists, and principally in the work of E. O. Wilson and his followers. The influence of these books and their claims has been very great, and the implications for the (apparently diminished) role of the humanities in a modern world are far reaching. It is now commonplace for human nature—the term, the concept, and the book title—to appear in conjunction with arguments concerning genetics, evolutionary psychology, and biological mating strategies of the human animal. Yet, as will become clear, the articulation of these arguments depends, both explicitly and implicitly, upon a use of categories, texts, and questions that have been inherited from the long history of the humanities.

E. O. Wilson begins his Pulitzer Prize-winning book, *On Human Nature* (1978), with an epigraph from Hume's *Inquiry Concerning Human Understanding* (1748), one of the grandest achievements of eighteenth-century philosophy:

> What though these reasonings concerning human nature seem abstract and of difficult comprehension, this affords no presumption of their falsehood. On the contrary, it seems impossible that what has hitherto escaped so many wise and profound philosophers can be very obvious and easy. And whatever pains these researches may cost us, we may think ourselves sufficiently rewarded, not only in point of profit but of pleasure, if, by that means, we can make any addition to our stock of knowledge in subjects of such unspeakable importance.

Wilson's own ruminations begin by taking up this quotation, and paraphrasing the questions that, he tells us, "the great philosopher David Hume said are of unspeakable importance: How does the mind work, and beyond that why does it work in such a way and not another, and from these two considerations together, what is man's ultimate nature?" For Wilson the last century of scientific inquiry, since Darwin, has altered expectations for any answers to these questions: "We are biological," he asserts. An acknowledgment of natural selection is "the essential first hypothesis for any serious consideration of the human condition":

> Without it the humanities and social sciences are the limited descriptors of surface phenomena, like astronomy without physics, biology without chemistry, and mathematics without algebra. With it, human nature can be laid open as an object of fully empirical research, biology can be put to the service of liberal education, and our self-conception can be enormously and truthfully enriched.[30]

The chapters of Wilson's book address in turn a series of topics that for him comprise a map of human nature: Heredity, Development, Emergence, Aggression, Sex, Altruism, Religion, and Hope. Here is a characteristically brilliant crescendo of generalization that displays Wilson comfortably astride his sociobiological hobbyhorse in a chapter entitled "Altruism":

Can the cultural evolution of higher ethical values gain a direction and momentum of its own and completely replace genetic evolution? I think not. The genes hold culture on a leash. The leash is very long, but inevitably values will be constrained in accordance with their effects on the human gene pool. The brain is a product of evolution. Human behavior—like the deepest capacities for emotional response which drive and guide it—is the circuitous technique by which human genetic material has been and will be kept intact. Morality has no other demonstrable ultimate function.[31]

Ethics and morality are byproducts of biological development, essentially defense mechanisms for keeping "human genetic material" intact. "Morality has no other demonstrable ultimate function." Philosophy is thus something like an optical illusion, as are poetry, fable, and aphorism. What we think are our "highest" functions are fully indebted to our "lowest"—to the body, to its self-preservation and circulation.

The glossary of terms appended to Wilson's book, which runs from *A* for *adaptation* to *Z* for *zoology,* pauses at the letter *H* (between *homozygous,* "when the genes located at a given site on [a] chromosome pair are identical to each other," and *hymenoptera,* "the insect order that contains all bees, wasps, and ants") to define *human nature* in a single pithy sentence:

> *Human nature.* In the broader sense, the full set of innate behavioral predispositions that characterize the human species; and in the narrower sense, those predispositions that affect social behavior.[32]

The key words here are *innate, behavioral, social,* and *predisposition.* A human being can act against his predisposition—biology is not destiny in a completely deterministic sense—but social, moral, and ethical practices have their underlying basis in the "nature" side of human nature. In a section called "Hope," Wilson calls for the development of what he calls a "biology of ethics," which will enable "the selection of a more deeply understood and enduring code of moral values." If dinosaurs had grasped the concept of "nobility," he suggests, "they might have survived. They might have been us."[33]

This is eloquent, and it is also troubling. What is the place of things like art, music, and poetry in Wilson's concept of human nature? Simply put, they are ornamental figures, illustrative metaphors deployed by a writer who has had a broad liberal education. "The processes of sexual pairbonding vary greatly among cultures, but they are everywhere steeped in emotional feeling," he writes. "In cultures with a romantic tradition, the attachment can be rapid and profound, creating love beyond sex which, once experienced, permanently alters the adolescent mind. Description of this part of human ethology is the refined specialty of poets, as we see in the remarkable expression by James Joyce." And at this point in his text Wilson quotes a long passage from Joyce's *Portrait of the Artist as a Young Man,* in which Stephen Daedalus sees a girl standing in the water who looks like a "strange and beautiful seabird."[34] It is not surprising that the naturalist's eye is caught by a figure of speech that invokes, and uses as its point of reference, an image from the natural world. The purely decorative role Wilson assigns to literature is clear in the fact that he does not footnote this passage, although he is careful to provide notes to all his scientific references, however glancing. (The notes are genteelly banished to the back of the book, signifying that *On Human Nature* is a piece of "philosophical" writing for the mainstream reader, not an insider text for scientists.)

Sometimes quoting literature out of context has inadvertent effects. Here is a telling example, from a discussion of "Group Selection and Altruism" in Wilson's 1980 classic, *Sociobiology:*

> Selection will discriminate against the individual if cheating has later adverse effects on his life and reproduction that outweigh the momentary advantage gained. Iago stated the essence in *Othello;* "Good name in man and woman, dear my lord, is the immediate jewel of their souls."[35]

There is no mention of Iago's position as the most arrant hypocrite in all of Shakespeare, nor of his own contempt for "good name" as compared to more material and vengeful rewards. Arguably "cheating" by Iago himself has later adverse effects on his life, since once his machinations are discovered he is led off in chains to be tortured at the play's close, but this does not seem to be the intent of the citation, which rather appears to aim at an endorsement of the sentiment expressed, despite the bad faith with which it is offered, in context, to the credulous Othello.

The literary references in *On Human Nature* tend to be less startling, but also more frequent. William Butler Yeats is invoked to support the belief, ascribed to "the reflective person," that "his life is in some incomprehensible manner guided through a biological ontogeny. . . . He senses that with all the drive, wit, love, pride, anger, hope, and anxiety that characterize the species he will in the end be sure only of helping to perpetuate the same cycle. Poets have defined this truth as tragedy. Yeats called it the coming of wisdom." Here Wilson inserts a four-line poem from Yeats, "The Coming of Wisdom with Time," in this case footnoted, but not commented upon within the text. The poetry is there to reinforce the cultural generalization. Again, and not surprisingly, the metaphors are drawn from the physical world, as if "truth" were a botanical effect:

> Though leaves are many, the root is one;
> Through all the lying days of my youth
> I swayed my leaves and flowers in the sun;
> Now I may wither into the truth.[36]

Yeats makes another brief appearance in Wilson's text ("what Yeats called the artifice of eternity") as do *Pilgrim's Progress* and a poem by Sappho, the latter again introduced with a now-familiar formula: "Poets have noted it well, as in the calm phrasing of Mary Barnard's [translation of] Sappho."[37] The poem is then quoted. I want here to call attention to the repetition of this move:

- "Description of this part of human ethology is the refined specialty of poets. . . ."
- "Poets have defined this truth as tragedy."
- "Poets have noted it well. . . ."

not only because of the supporting or cameo role in which it casts imaginative literature in its relationship to the quest for "human nature," but also because of the gauntlet that Wilson throws down toward the end of *On Human Nature,* in a passage in which he decries the *absence* of modern science and modern scientists from distinguished cultural conversations. Of all the assertions in his book, published in 1978, this peroration is perhaps the most surprising, since—in large part due to Wilson's own successes, and those of his students and disciplines—it is precisely science and scientists that now dominate the public conversation about human nature. Here is Wilson's long, passionate, and beautifully written conclusion:

> In the United States intellectuals are virtually defined as those who work in
> the prevailing mode of the social sciences and humanities. Their reflections
> are devoid of the idioms of chemistry and biology, as though humankind
> were still in some sense a numinous spectator of physical reality. In the pages
> of *The New York Review of Books, Commentary, The New Republic, Daedalus,*
> *National Review, Saturday Review,* and other literary journals articles dominate
> that read as if most of basic science had halted during the nineteenth century.
> Their content consists largely of historical anecdotes, diachronic collating of
> outdated, verbalized theories of human behavior, and judgments of current
> events according to personal ideology—all enlivened by the pleasant but
> frustrating techniques of effervescence. Modern science is still regarded as
> a problem-solving activity and a set of technical marvels, the importance of
> which is to be evaluated in an ethos extraneous to science. It is true that many
> "humanistic" scientists step outside scientific materialism to participate in the
> culture, sometimes as expert witnesses and sometimes as aspiring authors, but
> they almost never close the gap between the two worlds of discourse. With
> rare exceptions they are the tame scientists, the token emissaries of what must
> be viewed by their hosts as a barbaric culture still ungraced by a written lan-
> guage. They are degraded by the label they accept too readily: popularizers.
> Very few of the great writers, the ones who can trouble and move the deeper
> reaches of the mind, ever address real science on its own terms. Do they
> know the nature of the challenge?[38]

This is appropriately fierce, even though Wilson himself may at the end be looking

sideways in the mirror; he, after all, is both a "great writer" and a "popularizer," as

the success and esteem of this book and its author attest. In a later and equally ambi-

tious attempt at synthesis, a book entitled *Consilience* (literally "jumping together,"

or "concurrence," a term from the history of science),[39] he will say explicitly, "The

search for human nature can be viewed as the archaeology of the epigenetic rules."

In other words, fields that appear to be distinct from one another, like economics

and aesthetics, will be unified under this umbrella of genetic understanding. Science

will explain the humanities.

Many subsequent accounts of "human nature" have followed Wilson's lead,

filling the gap he lamented. In the years since Wilson's announcement of "sociobi-

ology" in the 1970s dozens of books and hundreds of articles have tried to account

for, or to rebut, the claim that human nature can be described, if not explained, by

science. Consider the title of a book by Kenan Malik: *Man, Beast and Zombie: What*

Science Can and Cannot Tell Us about Human Nature.[40] One of the most successful new books on this topic, Paul Ehrlich's *Human Natures: Genes, Cultures, and the Human Prospect,* stresses what Ehrlich, an evolutionary biologist, calls "cultural evolution." His book begins by asking "What is human nature?" He then goes on to explain why the term needs to be put in the plural: "'Human nature' as a singular concept embodies the erroneous notion that people possess a common set of rigid, genetically specified behavioral predilections that are unlikely to be altered by circumstances." But the study of human evolution in recent decades has taken account of behavioral flexibility and diversity in areas "as different as sexual preferences and political systems." Thus he resolves, "in light of this scientific progress," to "highlight human *natures:* the diverse and evolving behaviors, beliefs, and attitudes of *Homo sapiens.*"[41]

Ehrlich writes as a scientist, but he writes against "the extreme hereditary determinism that infests much of the current discussion of human behavior" and in favor of the ideas that biology has to be considered in the context of culture, and that "our culture is changing through an evolutionary process that is generally thought of as history."[42] Yet his book's references to philosophers (Immanuel Kant, Jürgen Habermas, Martin Heidegger, Charles Sanders Peirce, Richard Rorty) and poets (Samuel Taylor Coleridge, Percy Bysshe Shelley, J. W. von Goethe) appear almost exclusively in the footnotes, not in the text: humanities, literature, and the arts may underpin scientific observations but they are clearly secondary to his argument.[43] Ehrlich's notion of "cultural evolution," however politically progressive, still strongly emphasizes a theory of natural selection. (Characteristically, this softening of a brilliant and powerful paradigm, the shift from Wilson's uncompromising singular *nature* to Ehrlich's more affable plural, *natures,* robs the original insight of some of its force, even as it renders the evolutionary claims of sociobiology more acceptable to critical audiences.)

Of the host of other recent books by biologists on some aspect of human nature, most address questions of genetics, heredity, and evolution—and many bear enthusiastic blurbs by E. O. Wilson. Designed to cross over into the mainstream, these books have deliberately catchy titles. "*Mean Genes* is brilliant," Wilson writes of a book by Terry Burnham and Jay Phelan subtitled *From Sex to Money to Food: Taming Our Primal Instincts.* Burnham and Phelan, who have become talk-show favorites, take on such eye-catching topics as debt, fat, drugs, risk, greed, gender, beauty, infidelity, family, and friends and foes. "*Mean Genes* seeks to foster a deep understanding of human existence," they announce in the introduction. "The foundation of the book is evolutionary biology."[44] In *Are We Hardwired?* authors William R. Clark and Michael Grunstein address "the role of genes in human behavior," following in the controversial path of Richard Dawkins's *The Selfish Gene*.[45] Jared Diamond's *The Third Chimpanzee: The Evolution and Future of the Human Animal*, another Pulitzer Prize–winning study, asks, "What were those few key ingredients that made us human?" "*The Third Chimpanzee* will endure," the voice of Wilson asserts on the jacket flap, adding an evolutionary happy ending to the literary enterprise. In fact, though, Diamond's book is both a history and a warning, as is clear from the concluding section, entitled "Reversing Our Progress Overnight."

I might note that Diamond, like Wilson, occasionally uses a literary text to point a moral. Thus Shelley's "Ozymandias," a poem about a once-omnipotent king whose statue lies dismantled—a "colossal wreck"—in a desert wasteland, is quoted at the end of a chapter on golden ages. The inscription on the ruin's pedestal offers an inadvertently ironic commentary, since it too promises to "endure": "My name is Ozymandias, king of kings: Look on my works, ye mighty, and despair!"[46]

These are the books that E. O. Wilson wants to promote in the place of those by "tame scientists." All are clearly aimed at a general readership, and many have become best-sellers. What is most striking to me, as I have already briefly noted, is how completely the dominance in this discussion of human nature has swung around from the humanities to the sciences.

V

"Books," Jean-Paul Sartre wrote, "do serve some purpose. Culture doesn't save anything or anyone, it doesn't justify. But it's a product of man: he projects himself into it, he recognizes himself in it; that critical image alone offers him his image."[47] It seems to be human nature to *believe* in human nature, whatever those terms are taken to mean.

In point of fact, it is literature and the history of the imaginative arts that have *produced* "human nature." In the intellectual parlor game of "Man is the animal that . . ." (e.g., "man is a tool-using animal"; Spinoza's "man is a social animal"; Thomas Jefferson's "man is the only animal which devours his own kind") it is arguable that "man is the animal that speculates endlessly upon human nature," and that the history of that speculation, as much as any forensic tracing of cause and effect, is what constitutes the nature of human nature for our time.

Let me, then, return to my fundamental question: Why is "human nature" now, as it seems, firmly in the custody of biologists and evolutionary psychologists, on the one hand, and journalists, on the other? Why do so many of these books on "human nature" take as their subject politics, or social theory, or psychology, whether of the hard, soft, or pop variety? How can we account for the strong drift away from such questions by literary scholars and theorists, and by humanistic cultural critics?

The answers are not far to seek, and they are reasonable enough: multiculturalism, diversity, a respect for cultural difference, a suspicion of the politics of homogenization, a worry about coercive universalism. All of these critiques and displacements are worth taking very seriously, as any history of race relations, gender politics, religious intolerance, and patterns of immigration will make clear. But the reluctance of humanists to generalize on this topic—whether their reluctance is motivated by sophistication (there is no "we"), politics (the world is global and multicultural), or sheer weariness with what had become an inert and flabby cliché—has produced some unwelcome effects. In fact this may be a classic baby-and-bathwater scenario, in which humanists write themselves out of the story of who gets to describe and analyze "human nature."

There are, I want to suggest, three important reasons for the current estrangement between the humanities and human nature that deserve to be addressed. These reasons derive directly from the appropriation of the term by science and scientists, and before that by behaviorists and social scientists, and they can be summed up in three clunky words: *pluralization, verbalization,* and *interdisciplinarity.* Let me address them one by one.

- *Pluralization,* or the Fear of the Universal

The defensive pluralization of analytic concepts has become a hallmark of modern-day work, and speaks in part to commendable political concerns. The title of Paul Ehrlich's book is *Human Natures,* in the plural, and scholars of literature, anthropology, and cultural studies will all recall the move from "culture" to "cultures," as well as that from "history" to "histories," or indeed from "feminism" to "feminisms." But such welcome reminders about cultural difference are not without their inhibiting effects. One does not need to hanker after Bloom's magisterial *we* in order to recognize the value of structural analysis, generalization, and transhistorical analogy in the production of intellectually challenging theory—or theories. Humanists who find human nature either banal or imperialist should take another look, and see if there is a way of moving beyond the impasse of pluralization which has effectively blocked the way for a whole formal mode of literary and imagistic analysis.

Some insights in fact require one to be a dupe of universalism, because that is the only way fully to inhabit a culture. There are some things one cannot see from the outside, but only from within, even if that "within-ness" comes at the cost of a certain global overview. To speak plainly: pluralization may be good politics, but it produces undue deference to other disciplines, tacitly acknowledging that certain kinds of humanistic inquiry are elite, overspecialized, or without redeeming social value. It emphasizes historical context at the expense of synchronic relations within the work. It renders the specificity of language and the formal properties of art secondary, or ancillary, to local meaning. The opportunity for the humanities to lead rather than to remain secondary to the worlds of databases, experiments, and statistics is tied to the power to generalize and to speak and write cross-culturally. It necessarily involves combining the perspectives of inside and outside. The experience of the blindness produced by fully inhabiting a partial perspective is still the experience of "human life." This act of intellectual projection is too important a task to be left to the scientists, much less the social scientists, although humanists should welcome their collaboration.

• *Verbalization,* or the Fear of Taking Language Seriously

If we return for a moment to E. O. Wilson's final remarks in *On Human Nature*—remarks as powerful as they are provocative—we can take another look at his perfectly justifiable put-down of journalistic attempts to talk science: "their content consists largely of historical anecdotes, diachronic collating of outdated, *verbalized* theories of human behavior, and judgments of current events according to personal ideology" (emphasis added). Here I want to single out the word *verbalized,* which seems to bear a lot of negative weight: *to verbalize* in this context is to translate, and translate badly, from one language, the language of science, into another language, the language of journalism and popular discourse. *Verbalize* here is cognate to terms like *intellectualize* and *rationalize*—words that suggest that the activity in question is a second-order phenomenon, a stage removed from the thing itself. What Wilson admires in language is its beauty, its decorative capacity. In another telling phrase, he insists that without taking biology into account "the humanities and social sciences are the limited descriptors of surface phenomena," like astronomy without physics, biology without chemistry, and mathematics without algebra.

"Limited descriptors of surface phenomena"—it is hard to think of a more genteelly damning phrase. But the phrase itself is a "limited descriptor," which betrays its own bias.

For humanists, verbalization cannot be so simple a process: language is itself the object of our analysis, the thing itself, and it is the inherent (neither "natural" nor "unnatural") tensions within language, the powerful instabilities of meaning, that make up for many humanistic scholars and writers the core material out of which any interesting theory of "human nature" might derive. A similar fate, incidentally, has befallen the word *literacy,* which—transformed into social-betterment formulas such as "cultural literacy" and "moral literacy"—has lost its direct connection with the difficult and dangerous act of reading.

"What shall we call human in humans," asks Lyotard, "the initial misery of their childhood, or their capacity to acquire a 'second' nature which, thanks to language, makes them fit to share in communal life, adult consciousness and reason? That the second depends on and presupposes the first is agreed by everyone. The question is only that of knowing whether this dialectic, whatever name we grace it with, leaves no remainder."[48]

- *Interdisciplinarity,* or the Return of Human Nature

Over the last several years a number of new interdisciplinary fields have grown up, and others previously in existence have expanded and prospered. Such areas as the history of science and technology, cognitive theory and the arts, and visual anthropology, are interdisciplinary both in method and in scope, crossing boundaries between and among the humanities, the social sciences, and the sciences. Visual anthropology, to use one example, takes as material for analysis elements like ethnographic film, photography, mass media, and other anthropological "ways of seeing."

Fields like this attract younger scholars in great numbers: majors in these areas are increasing. So many interdisciplinary dissertations are being written—and interdisciplinary courses being taught—that it is sometimes difficult to guess which department is the host of a course in, for example, Fraud and Intellectual Property (History of Science); Eighteenth-Century Ethical Dilemmas (Romance Languages and Literatures); Culture, Politics, and Media (Anthropology); or Literature, Science, and Technology in the Nineteenth Century (English). These are all courses taught at Harvard College today. Fraud, ethics, games, media, science and technology: this is a pretty fair glossary of terms for "human nature." And these are just courses randomly picked from one college course catalogue, where dozens of other course catalogues might tell the same story.

Of course, by this time "interdisciplinarity" is not news. It has its proponents and its skeptics, and the latter include many people who believe that a professional training, or even a degree, is a necessary passport for anyone seeking to embark upon research in a field. We may note that the absence of such a degree in, say, literature, philosophy, or the history of art, has not deterred physicists and biologists from saying wise things about poetry en passant. This lack of equity between the sciences and the humanities—the idea that we can all speak about literature, and that, in fact, a professional discourse about literary studies renders the work in that field arcane and obstructive—is part of the problem about the current custody of "human nature"; for the very existence and prominence of interdisciplinary studies in the narrative fields suggests that an interest in human nature has survived, and returned, in those fields. It has, of course, staged its comeback stealthily, as was necessary, lest it be laughed off the platform. But this is human nature with a difference—human nature approached, as it were, from within and from below, rather than magisterially from above.

Interdisciplinarity, we could say—borrowing one term from E. O. Wilson and another from contemporary political philosophy—is *consilience* without *hegemony*. Or, to speak more plainly, it is mutually respectful collaborative work among the disciplines (largely but not exclusively the discursive and narrative disciplines, the humanities, and the less-quantitative branches of science and social science). Interdisciplinarity, in short, is the space, or the mode of collective inquiry, where questions about "human nature" are *now,* at present, being investigated. And this makes perfect sense. It explains, in part, the dissatisfaction with the boundaries of the present-day disciplines, for breaching boundaries—arguably a natural human desire—is not in itself sufficient to explain this explosion of integrated interests. The old-fashioned questions about human nature, ethics and morality, idealization and expression, and humankind's reaching close to the angels and the beasts are accommodated in new places and new guises by interdisciplinary inquiry. Thus, for example, the release of a new film version of *Planet of the Apes* (2000) provoked a discussion of the relationship of humans and chimpanzees, orangutans, gorillas, and bonobos, and led to an interesting exchange of views among animal behaviorists, theoretical biologists, anthropologists, and lawyers on the question of rights for apes.[49]

But the humanities have a single, easy-to-forget point to repeat over and over in these intellectual investigations. Language is not a secondary but a primary constituent of human nature, whatever may turn out to be the case in other spheres. Language is not transparent, though fantasies of its transparency, its merely denotative role, have always attracted and misled some of its users, both writers and readers. Language is not only a window but also a door, a barrier as well as a portal, requiring a handle—and a key.

It is precisely because no one kind of inquiry holds the key to "human nature" that interdisciplinary groupings form and re-form. The humanities sometimes play an ironic role in this by appearing to pose a set of framing illusions that science can demystify. But this is true only from the perspective of the humanities themselves. Scientists often take pleasure in demonstrating that William Shakespeare was right about human nature, even though he had no access to modern scientific information. They are frequently impatient, or uncomprehending, about the work of humanists who question the sources, the sincerity, and the consistency of a "Shakespeare" who is to a certain extent the creation of editors, poets, and critics who lived long after his time. Far from demystifying categories like truth and beauty, scientists often write as if the humanities could still be relied upon to be the quaint but lovable guardians of such notions. In this sense many scientists retain a nineteenth-century notion of the humanities, even as they suggest that humanists cling to a nineteenth-century notion of science.

When a leading scientist like E. O. Wilson could aver that "[m]odern science is still regarded as a problem-solving activity and a set of technical marvels, the importance of which is to be valuated in an ethos extraneous to science," it is well worth asking him to consider the obverse of this proposition: that modern humanistic study is all too often regarded as a style-enhancing activity and a set of linguistic tricks, the importance of which is to be evaluated in an ethos extraneous to the humanities.

As the popularity of programs in the history of science and technology suggests, science itself has a history, and, in the very nature of such things, it is a history of falsehoods in pursuit of truth. The philosopher Miguel de Unamuno put it clearly when he wrote, "Science is a cemetery of dead ideas, even though life may issue from them," and, "True science teaches, above all, to doubt and to be ignorant."[50] From the Ptolemaic universe (the sun rotates around the earth) to phlogiston (the hypothetical substance supposed to be the "matter of fire," whose existence was affirmed through much of the eighteenth century only to be rejected and abandoned by 1800), science has proceeded by hypothesis, by theory, and by inspired accident and guess. The "beautiful theories" of the past have become either facts or follies. Will today's answers be any more ahistorical, transcendent, and permanent than all those that have gone before?

It is striking that the term "science wars" has been coined to describe the efforts on the part of some nonscience scholars to understand how scientists construct their notions of truth. The term itself has been highly contestatory, producing heated exchanges and a good deal of willful misunderstanding on all sides. What I have been describing here might perhaps have been called "humanities wars," save for the fact that the humanities are regarded not as specialized knowledge or even as a research field, but rather as the ground of our common knowledge and common inheritance, accessible to scientists, social scientists, and humanists alike. Instead of "humanities wars," then, we have the far more aversive "culture wars," as if the progress of scholarship in the humanities was itself a "war" against, as well as for custody of, certain cultural values and touchstones that are thought to be enshrined in literature and art. I share with Ian Hacking a dislike of the facile use of "war" to describe these intellectual debates. As he says, expressions like "culture wars," "science wars," and "Freud wars" suggest gladiatorial contests, in which the pleasure—and the "war" terminology—belongs to "the bemused spectators."[51] But somewhat obscured by the inflammatory rhetoric, fanned by the flames of cultural journalists, is a fundamental dissymmetry in the way "scientific knowledge" and "humanistic knowledge" are weighed, valued, and assessed.

Is it really necessary to ban all scientific experimentation in order to preserve human nature as a constant and unchanging essence? Francis Fukuyama's concern that contemporary biotechnology will "alter human nature and thereby move us into a 'posthuman' stage of history," with "possibly malign consequences for liberal democracy and the nature of politics,"[52] is one that has in fact been contemplated, sans alarm, by many thoughtful scholars in various branches of the humanities, where "posthuman" is not a scare word but an interesting field for philosophical, ethical, and aesthetic speculation. Perhaps we need the humanities more than ever precisely because it is so obvious that scientific progress cannot be stopped. Here is where humanists can do themselves, and the world, a favor, by stressing the ways in which all knowledge is an aspect of rhetoric as well as an aspect of logic. Increasingly, scientists speak in metaphors and linguistic coinages in order to explain their work. *Relativity; quark; revolution; game theory; prisoner's dilemma:* these appropriations of language, analogy, and neologism enrich understanding by becoming figural, by pointing out that the reality of the world itself is a voiced reality, a reality of figure. Humanists might reasonably point out the rhetorical and "poetic" nature of these terms, the impossibility of science without image and figure. But at the same time these humanists also might return the serve, and the favor, by laying claim once again to the most underrated and overliteralized of these figures: the metaphor of human nature.

So, to restate the question with which we have been wrestling: why is it that today's scientists write about human nature, while today's humanists do not? My answer, at least in part, is that humanists *do* write about this question, constantly, but that neither they nor many of their readers—not to mention their critics—have been willing to acknowledge that that is what they are doing. Somewhere along the way, the concept of human nature became both stale and saccharine: a set of bromides or truisms, often inflected with religion and frequently invoked as a "so there" pseudo-explanation ("it's just human nature . . . ") rather than explored as a conundrum or a puzzlement.

    I am eager here—or, to be franker about it, I am anxious—not to be heard as deploring the present moment in humanistic writing and research, and harking back, wistfully, to a time when men were men, women were women, and humanists cared about human nature. My point is really close to the opposite of this nostalgic and retrogressive thought: what I have been contending is that today's humanists are asking "human nature" questions all the time, when they talk about psychic violence, or material culture, or epistemic breaks, or the history of the book, or the counterintuitive. Many of the theoretical explorations and innovations of the last fifty years of humanistic scholarship have been aimed at demystifying a unitary and positivistic sense of "human nature." But to aim to demystify something is tacitly to acknowledge its mystified status, and not only for others; also for oneself. Avoiding the topic of "human nature" is a mistake, one that has political as well as intellectual ramifications—a mistake based on underestimating what and how we read and write today. Like Edgar Allan Poe's famous image of the continental map, with letters so large that we cannot read the most overarching words (Europe, Africa) and focus instead on the legible terms in smaller print (Geneva, New Jersey), the terrain on which we work, the terrain inscribed by its own name and ours, is bizarrely unreadable to us. Yet "human nature," as a term and as a field of inquiry, need not be solely the concern of social conservatives or of scientists, however well meaning and however well placed. In debunking all the illusions fostered under this ubiquitous term, contemporary humanistic scholars have sometimes failed to see in what ways we are working within it.

When I suggest that to discard a big and baggy idea like human nature is a political mistake, what I mean is that it has given aid and comfort to unthinking critics of the humanities. If we are willing to reflect seriously and critically, we will readily be able to demonstrate that fields like cultural anthropology, structural linguistics, women's studies, cybertheory, and posthumanism are indeed addressing the Big Questions: the Who Am I questions, the What Am I Doing Here questions, the What Lies in the Future questions that all attach themselves to the heritage of "human nature." These questions, indeed, have never been more pressing—nor more "human"—than they are today.

1   Madeleine Bunting, "The Morning After," *Guardian* (London), 12 September 2001, 14.

2   Joelle Sumner, John F. Kennedy High School, Bellmore, N.Y., "Student Briefing Page on the News," *Newsday* (Long Island, N.Y.), 4 October 2001, A24.

3   Mimi Avins and Cara Mia DiMassa, "Amid Disaster, Heroes Ran toward Danger, Not from It," *Los Angeles Times*, 21 September 2001, sec. 5, p. 1.

4   Nicholas M. Christian, Glenn Collins, Jim Dwyer, Joseph P. Fried, Jan Hoffman, Mireya Nvarro, Maria Newman, Mirta Ojito, Barbara Stewart, and Joyce Wadler, "A Nation Challenged: The Missing," *New York Times*, 2 October 2001, B9.

5   Madeleine Bunting, "The Launch of a TV Game that Trades on our Dark Side," *Guardian* (London), 21 May 2001, 20.

6 Joyce Purnick, "Intern's Role Appears to Be Same Sad Tale," *New York Times,* 12 July 2001, B1.

7 Francine Prose, "The Big Surprise? Our Surprise," *Washington Post,* 18 February 2001, B1.

8 Quoted in Ellen Gamerman, "Hillary Clinton, Fund-raiser," *Baltimore Sun,* 25 April 2001, 1A.

9 George F. Will, "A Principled Solution to Stem Cell Dilemma," *Baltimore Sun,* 16 April 2001, 19A.

10 Karl Marx, "Introduction to a Critique of Political Economy," in Marx and Frederick Engels, *The German Ideology,* ed. C. J. Arthur (New York: International Publishers, 1974), 124.

11 Anna Quindlen, *A Short Guide to a Happy Life* (New York: Random House, 2000), 124.

12 Ken Karnofsky, "Genome Project Can't Explain Human Nature," Letters to the Editor, *Boston Globe,* 16 February 2001, A18.

13 Editorial, "Mysteries of the Genes," *New York Times,* 17 February 2001, A30.

14 Francis Fukuyama, *Our Posthuman Future* (New York: Farrar, Straus and Giroux, 2002), 83.

15 Jared Diamond, *The Third Chimpanzee* (New York: Harper Perennial, 1992), 137.

16 From the Arden Shakespeare edition (London and New York: Routledge, 1993). All further Shakespeare citations are from this edition.

17 Clifford Geertz, *The Interpretation of Cultures* (New York: Basic Books, 1973), 67.

18 Marx, "Introduction to a Critique of Political Economy," 124.

19 J. Stanley Grimes, *The Mysteries of Human Nature Explained by a New System of Nervous Physiology, To Which Is Added, a Review of the Errors of Spiritualism, and Instructions for Developing or Refining the Influence by Which Subjects and Mediums Are Made* (Buffalo: R. M. Wanzer, 1857); Louis Berman, *The Glands Regulating Personality: A Study of the Glands of Internal Secretion in Relation to the Types of Human Nature* (New York: Macmillan, 1921), viii.

20 Berman, *The Glands Regulating Personality,* 21, 23, 26, 329.

21 John Dewey, *Human Nature and Conduct* (Madison, Wisc.: Henry Holt, 1944), 113–14.

22 Ibid.

23 Virginia Woolf, *The Common Reader* (1925; reprint, New York: Harcourt, Brace and Company, 1984), 63, 93, 137, 167.

24 T. S. Eliot, *Selected Essays 1917–1932* (New York: Harcourt, Brace and Company, 1932), 111, 158, 279.

25 Harold Bloom, *Shakespeare: The Invention of the Human* (New York: Riverhead Books, 1998), 1, 17.

26 Hannah Arendt, *The Human Condition,* 2d ed. (Chicago: University of Chicago Press, 1998), 11.

27 Jean-François Lyotard, *The Inhuman: Reflections on Time,* trans. Geoffrey Bennington and Rachel Bowlby (Cambridge: Polity Press, 1991), 2.

28 Robert Pepperell, *The Post-Human Condition* (Oxford: Intellect, 1995), i.

29 E. O. Wilson, *On Human Nature* (Cambridge, Mass.: Harvard University Press, 1978), 2.

30 Ibid.

31 Ibid., 167.

32 Ibid., 281.

33 Ibid., 196, 197.

34　Ibid., 69.

35　E. O. Wilson, *Sociobiology* (Cambridge, Mass.: Belknap Press of Harvard University Press, 1980), 58.

36　Quoted by Wilson, *On Human Nature*, 3. Reprinted with permission from *The Collected Poems of W. B. Yeats* (New York: Macmillan, 1940), 92.

37　Wilson, *On Human Nature*, 200.

38　Ibid., 203.

39　William Whewell, *The Philosophy of the Inductive Sciences*, vol. 6, part 2, ed. G. Buchdahl and L. L. Sauden (London: Frank Cass and Co. Ltd., 1967), 65 (originally published 1840): "[T]he cases in which inductions from classes of facts altogether or different have thus *jumped together*, belong only to the best established theories that the history of science contains . . . . [I] will term it the *Consilience of Inductions*."

40　Kenan Malik, *Man, Beast and Zombie: What Science Can and Cannot Tell Us about Human Nature* (New York: Weidenfeld, 2000).

41　Paul Ehrlich, *Human Natures* (Washington, D.C.: Island Press, 2000), ix.

42　Ibid., x.

43　Even these footnotes are of the most perfunctory and summary kind: a "romantic response" to Enlightenment science, representing "a preference for feeling, intuition, imagination, and self-expression over rational analysis and intellect," is said to be "associated with such writers and thinkers as German philosopher Friedrich von Schelling and Johann von Goethe, Johann von Schiller, Samuel Taylor Coleridge, and Percy Bysshe Shelley" (426 n. 73). This is the sort of thing one finds in readers' encyclopedias and school texts; a generalization this un-nuanced from a literary critic speaking about science would surely evoke protests from scientific theorists and practitioners.

44　Terry Burnham and Jay Phelan, *Mean Genes* (Cambridge, Mass.: Perseus, 2000), 8.

45　William R. Clark and Michael Grunstein, *Are We Hardwired?* (New York: Oxford University Press, 2000).

46　Quoted in Diamond, *The Third Chimpanzee*, 338.

47　Jean-Paul Sartre, *Les Mots* (The Words), trans. Bernard Frechtman (New York: G. Braziller, 1964), 254.

48　Lyotard, *The Inhuman*, 3.

49　Rowan Taylor of the Great Ape Project, quoted in Seth Mydans, "He's Not Hairy, He's My Brother," *New York Times*, 12 August 2001, sec. 4, p. 5.

50　Miguel de Unamuno, *Tragic Sense of Life*, trans. J. E. Crawford Fitch (New York: Dover Publications, 1954), 90, 93.

51　Ian Hacking, *The Social Construction of What?* (Cambridge, Mass.: Harvard University Press, 1999), 4.

52　Fukuyama, *Our Posthuman Future*, 7.

Historical Correctness:

The Use and Abuse of History for Literature

*The unhistorical and the historical are necessary in equal measure
for the health of an individual, of a people and of a culture.*

FRIEDRICH NIETZSCHE,
"ON THE USES AND DISADVANTAGES OF HISTORY FOR LIFE"

—What useful discovery did Socrates learn from Xanthippe?
—Dialectic, Stephen answered.

JAMES JOYCE, *ULYSSES*

I

We who profess literary studies have been living through a time of infatuation with history. This is not the first such crush, to be sure, but it is a heady one. And like all infatuations, it carries with it a certain overestimation of the object. History seems to know everything that we want to know, and to offer "answers" to knotty textual questions: questions of context, interpretation, and indeed meaning. Earlier in this century articles and footnotes about *Macbeth* lay emphasis on the facts of the Gunpowder Plot and the lineage of James I. An entire mini-industry in what might be called "Essex Studies" grew up around the Earl of Essex, his marital connection to the circle of Sir Philip Sidney and his sister the Countess of Pembroke, and his ill-fated rebellion—all in service of readings, not only of Shakespeare's history plays, but also of his tragedies, comedies, and romances. Readings of *The Merchant of Venice* still routinely incorporate the unhappy story of Queen Elizabeth's Jewish doctor, Roderigo Lopez, and, informed by a growing interest in race, analyses of *Othello* detail the numbers and social occupations of Moors and Africans in sixteenth-century London.

But where these inquiries focused on political history, today's scholars of early modern literature and culture are more likely to turn to conduct books, mothers' manuals, and medical and rhetorical treatises. We have seen in recent years an intense interest in court culture, literacy and reading practices, the printing house, sexuality and the stage, and witchcraft and colonial encounters, all "grounded in material and social determinants."[1] This is the counterpart of the earlier infatuation on the part of historians for literary theory, the so-called "linguistic turn"—a passion now strenuously disavowed, like so many other love affairs gone wrong. Whereas historians were once struck by the nontransparency of their medium and the need to study it rather than simply to look at the past through it, today's literary scholars are fascinated by the task of reconstructing "the real" that must lie behind any of its representations.

My topic is the way that "history" has emerged as a byword for a certain kind of truth-claim in literary studies. New Historicism, nourished and nurtured

by interdisciplinary work, by historians and art historians as well as by literary critics, had an enormous impact upon the way emerging younger scholars taught and
wrote about literature in the late twentieth century. But the very point that New
Historicism tried to stress—that history, or histories, could not be understood as
determinative or lineal causes but rather as complex networks of cultural effects—
has been eroded by its success. Spawned by postmodernism, New Historicism tried
to avoid or complicate causality: it preferred words such as *resonance, circulation, poet-
ics,* and *social energy.* But through its very avoidances this strategy whetted the appetite
for causation. To put it another way, New Historicism began by reading history as
a text, but it created, despite its best efforts, a desire for history as a ground. In the
wake of postmodernism and the general questioning of foundations, a longing to
find causality—the priority of history, history as explanation—seems to have come
back to literary study more strongly than before. For many scholars of literature,
causality is the unfulfilled desire, the projected or introjected fantasy, the prohib-
ited wish. The question these scholars ask is often a version of *why*—not a version
of *how.*

Indeed, recent critiques of New Historicism have taken it to task for not
being historical *enough:* it is faulted for "its anecdotal notion of what counts as history; its dependence on loose analogies; its evasiveness when it comes to causal argument; its tendency to adduce a Zeitgeist from an accident," as one friendly critic has
put it.[2] In other words, precisely what distinguishes New Historicism from history,
its interest in "the literary," has seemed to some scholars—both historians and literary scholars—to be its weakness rather than its strength.

It occurs to me that some readers might take the title of this essay to refer
to the need for "historical correctness," as implied by a headline in the *New York
Times:* "We Happy Many, Playing Fast and Loose with History." The point of that
article was that although Shakespeare, like many modern artists and writers, did manip-
ulate history, he had a more nuanced, complex, and learned way of doing so than,
for example, director Oliver Stone, or actor-director Tim Robbins. "Shakespeare
approached history with depth and integrity," insists the *Times* reviewer. "The con-
tract that he made with his viewers was that they were witnessing an interpretation

of history, not an exact reproduction of events. Most historical movies, by contrast, not only reduce history to a simple situation but also strive to give the impression that they are reconstructing what really happened."[3] Whatever the truth value of this distinction—and it does become muddier as time goes on, as Shakespeare's plays are all that many modern nonhistorians know about English or even Roman history—it is not in fact precisely what I mean by "historical correctness." For I intend here to invoke the cognate phrase "political correctness," one of the most denigrated and vilified imperatives in contemporary journalism and academic life.

Political correctness in today's popular parlance is understood to mean an insensitive attack on insensitivity. With its roots in old-style totalitarian discourse (as early as 1947 Vladimir Nabokov could mock it in his novel *Bend Sinister*[4]) the phrase was used in the 1970s with heavy self-irony by the left as a kind of amused reality check on its own excesses, and often abbreviated by its initials as a sign of this ruefully affectionate self-estrangement. Perhaps inevitably, the term was picked up by the Right, denuded of any soupçon of irony, and used as a club to beat those very persons who had ironized it to begin with.[5] "Political correctness" is rather old and rather tired news in the United States, where it tends to be employed principally by diehard cultural conservatives and the authors of novels and plays about academic life. A review of *The Winter's Tale* at the American Repertory Theater scolded the director for adding "a politically correct ending," noting that "it is political correctness to disallow Shakespeare's forgiveness."[6]

European commentators often consider political correctness a symptom of both American puritanism and feminist excess. Thus a French book on the history of flirting deplores the "return to puritanism" and the rise of sexual harassment laws, insisting that "there is nothing politically incorrect in a little ambiguous banter between men and women." In Britain "political correctness" has been decried in the press as having "some of the characteristics of a religious sect." When a popular judge at the Old Bailey stepped down from the bench he did so in a highly publicized speech that inveighed against a new conduct book for judges on how to avoid the perception of racial bias and against "political correctness in all its horrid forms."[7] Horrid or not, political correctness has been regarded as a tendency to turn critique into a new orthodoxy or orthopedic thinking, framing and shaping what can be thought and said.

What, then, is "historical correctness"? We might say that it is the suggestion, either implied or explicit, on the part of literary scholars, that history grounds and tells the truth about literature. The critique of this idea is superbly well made by Walter Benjamin's remark at the end of an essay called "Literary History and the Study of Literature":

> What is at stake is not to portray literary works in the context of their age, but to represent the age that perceives them—our age—in the age during which they arose. It is this that makes literature into an organon of history; and to achieve this, and not to reduce literature to the material of history, is the task of the literary historian.[8]

II

The most specifically *literary* charge offered against those who do not read historically or who deliberately and joyously flout chronology and sequence is the charge of anachronism—in effect, historical *in*correctness. Anachronism, from the Greek for "back" and "time," has itself had a chequered history. As the neglect or falsification of chronological relation, whether intentional or not, it is often regarded merely as a vulgar error. A clock strikes in the Rome of Shakespeare's *Julius Caesar*. An attendant to the Pharaoh in Cecil B. DeMille's *The Ten Commandments* appears in tennis shoes. In the canonical history of art and literature anachronisms are frequent, and some have been naturalized over the years in the service of "timeless" art or the double time of revealed truth. The *sacra conversazione* of Renaissance religious painting brings together Madonna, Christ child, angels, saints, and contemporary donors from the artist's time in a single transhistorical space. In northern European art you may encounter Joseph hard at work in a fifteenth-century shop, or the Virgin Mary as a Netherlandish burgher's daughter. In Florence or in Naples she is an Italian peasant girl. The Belgian painter James Ensor depicts, in 1880, Christ's entry into Brussels.

In literature we find similar "errors," often deliberately contrived for effect.

Dido and Aeneas are made contemporaries by Virgil, though they lived three hundred years apart. Shakespeare famously alters history from time to time. He depicts King Duncan of Scotland as an elderly and beloved monarch, rather than the younger and feebler ruler described in Raphael Holinshed's *Chronicles*. He makes his two Harrys, Harry Percy and Harry Monmouth, age-mates rather than a generation apart. He describes the historical Cleopatra, a mere twenty-nine years old when his play opens, as "wrinkled deep in time." In *Titus Andronicus,* a Goth from the time of the Roman Empire pauses "to gaze upon a ruinous monastery" (5.1.121), thus invoking the Reformation context and Henry VIII's dissolution of the monasteries.[9] Mark Twain places a Connecticut Yankee in King Arthur's court. Thornton Wilder moves a single set of characters through a variety of geological and historical periods from paleolithic to modern in his play *The Skin of Our Teeth.* In each of these cases a point is being made about the present day.

Yet often artists and writers are criticized for their anachronisms, like the Gothic novelist Ann Radcliffe or the Roman historian Sallust. In these instances *anachronism* becomes conflated with sloppiness or ignorance rather than with aesthetic, political, or satirical effect. The Hollywood speciality known as "continuity" is meant to clean up such inadvertent errors. Forgeries in films are often detected, or detectable, by unwitting anachronisms: too many stars on the U.S. flag, the wrong period fashion in dress or hair, a telephone in the "Old West" saloon, a piece of advanced technology out of its time and place. The two faces of anachronism (deliberate juxtaposition to make a clever point; awkward and revealing error of fact) are often regarded as different in kind as well as degree. It is the bugbear of "intentionality" again: a knowing error is a cleverness, an unknowing error is a *bêtise.* But it is sometimes hard to tell the difference. DeMille's *Ten Commandments* stages a Passover celebration that vastly postdates the time of the Biblical event, presenting a modern-looking rabbinic seder rather than a lamb sacrifice. Joseph L. Mankiewicz's version of Shakespeare's *Julius Caesar* (1953) features portrait busts that closely resemble the Emperor Hadrian, who was born about a century and a half later. Joseph von Sternberg's 1934 film *The Scarlet Empress* offers Marlene Dietrich in the role of Catherine the Great. The soundtrack of this film about eighteenth-century Russia included the music of Mendelssohn, Tchaikovsky (including the *1812 Overture*), Rimsky-Korsakov, and Wagner's "Ride of the Valkyries."[10] Such anachronisms could be inadvertent or deliberate: whether intended or not, they tell us something about the moment of production and consumption. *Anachronism* in this sense is another term for *bricolage*.

Kathleen Coleman, a professor of Latin and an expert on Roman games, was hired as a consultant to the film *Gladiator* (2000), and found it "an interesting but ultimately disillusioning experience." No sooner did she set the historical record straight, she noted, than "a whole range of fresh inaccuracies and anachronisms" crept in and were immortalized on film, including fictive inscriptions in bad Latin engraved upon the public buildings. Misunderstanding Juvenal's phrase "bread and circuses," the placating of the hungry and discontented masses with public spectacles like chariot races, the filmmakers invented a slew of imperial caterers tossing bread into the stadium stands.[11] "*Gladiator* ain't history," wrote Philip Howard jauntily in the London *Times*. "Its account of Roman politics is nonsense. Marcus Aurelius never dreamt of restoring power to the people. . . . The heroic general Maximus with republican dreams in the film is a John Wayne fantasy. The Senate gave up any republican inclinations long before." Howard found "the anachronism [he] most enjoyed" was Maximus praying to the shade of his murdered son, and advising him to keep his heels down when riding. "Since the Romans had not yet cribbed the stirrup from the Goths, this was seriously foolish advice." And modern culture, it seems, has the thumbs up/thumbs down gesture backward. "When the crowd in the Colosseum wanted a popular gladiator to be spared they turned their thumbs down into their fists. Thumbs up meant 'Cut his throat,'" Howard explained. (Readers seeking corroboration for this point may consult Montaigne's essay "Of Thumbs."[12]) Nonetheless, Howard liked the film, which he thought embodied modern as well as ancient tastes for blood sport, from boxing to professional football. As he noted, "We continually reinvent the past to match our present concerns, causes and totems."[13]

Nor is the allure of anachronism a new development, a mere artifact of modern or postmodern life. The fashion for dialogues with the dead, modeled after Lucian, provided the opportunity for explicitly anachronistic interchange: Fontanelle's *New Dialogues of the Dead* (*Nouveaux dialogues des morts,* 1683–1684) offered dialogues between Socrates and Montaigne, Seneca and Scarron. Fénelon's *Dialogues des morts* (1700–1718) followed the same pattern, as did English writers like Walter Savage Landor, whose *Imaginary Conversations* (1824) included colloquies between Achilles and Helen, Galileo and John Milton, the Earl of Essex and Edmund Spenser, Joan of Arc and Agnes Sorel.

A memorable instance of this once-popular genre was offered by comedian Steve Allen's television show *Meeting of Minds,* which ran for four years on the American Public Broadcasting System. On one occasion Aristotle, Sun Yat-Sen, Niccolò Machiavelli, and Elizabeth Barrett Browning debated; on another a lively argument developed among Theodore Roosevelt, Thomas Aquinas, Cleopatra, and Thomas Paine; a third panel featured Florence Nightingale, Plato, Voltaire, and Martin Luther; a fourth, Attila the Hun, Emily Dickinson, Galileo, and Charles Darwin. (Steve Allen to Galileo: "You know, it's most interesting. You sir, Miss Dickinson, and Dr. Darwin all had difficulty with domineering fathers." Attila: "My father, too, was no bargain." Or Karl Marx to Marie Antoinette, from a panel discussion with Ulysses S. Grant, Marie Antoinette, Thomas More, and Marx: "Did it ever enter your mind, Your Majesty, that . . . empty rituals and customs would in time destroy the people's respect for the monarchy?" Marie: "Nonsense, Dr. Marx, the people adored the rituals and customs!" Thomas More: "Yes, Dr. Marx, . . . rituals and manners aided the people to express their respect for royalty. I understand that in today's Marxist nations there is still room for pomp and circumstance.")[14] These were not séances; actors played the parts. Allen's wife Jayne Meadows performed almost all the female roles.[15]

The pleasure opened up by such deliberate violations of history seems somehow old-fashioned today. But why should that be? What was being disregarded then— or now? Are we simply too conscious of history to be playful in this way? Is there something about the interest in history and politics that gives anachronism a bad name? Or is anachronism simply returning in a new form? A useful analogue to this problem can be found in the current "antichronology" debates among art historians, curators, and art critics—debates inflamed by the thematic, nonchronological installations at such high-profile museums as the Tate Modern, the Tate Britain, the Museum of Modern Art, and the Brooklyn Museum. As art historian Linda Nochlin has noted, "[T]here is a tendency to use chronology as teleology." A "nonchronological hang," she suggested, can "break up the idea of an uninterrupted flow."[16] But other critics have objected, perceiving the loss of chronology as a loss of coherence. Thus for example British art critic David Sylvester thought the Tate Modern's decision to follow themes rather than periods was a mistake; chronology, he argued, was "an objective reality, built into the fabric of the work," not "a tool of art-historical interpretation which can be used at one moment and discarded at another."[17]

What was at stake here? Chronology implied evolution and a certain kind of progress narrative, privileging some works and movements above others. History was a history of aesthetic forms: their development and evolution was the ground of meaningful art history. Antichronology (dismissed in some quarters as political correctness because it shifted the focus away from "masterpieces") drew attention to merely looking. It invited pleasure and irresponsibility, not the accuracy of any story. Antichronology, then, is both old and new: both a resistance to an older notion of historical sequence and development and a rediscovery of familiar categories like genre, theme, and structure. These categories were not simply resurrected; they were substantially altered, as for example in the notion of many alternative modernisms rather than one.[18] But their chief effect was to open up some kinds of interpretation that might have been closed off by chronology. Placing a Rembrandt next to a Mark Rothko or a Norman Rockwell raises issues of similarity and difference, form and mood, which neither chronology nor historical context will address or ground.

This suggests another sense in which the word *anachronism* has been used to criticize and control a development in literary studies: the anachronism not within the text itself but within the framework used to read it. In some ways, of course, the question of history's value for literature is an old and familiar debate. In a 1910 essay called "Anachronism in Shakespeare Criticism," the literary scholar Elmer Edgar Stoll lamented that "Criticism forgets that Shakespeare wrote in the sixteenth century," turning him instead into a "twentieth-century symbolist." (The tension here was partly one between "scholars" and "critics," the latter excoriated as "poets, essayists, gentlemen of taste and leisure, not to mention a horde of the tasteless and leisureless—propagandists and blatherskites.") Stoll's chief culprit was character criticism and psychology, which he thought wildly inappropriate for the discussion of Elizabethan literature. The issue, in short, was one of what I have called respect: respect for sixteenth-century ideas about the preeminence of story and plot, in contrast with "our modern ideas" of character and social problems.

It was anachronistic, Stoll said, to regard Shakespeare as having any interest in "the newer psychology concerning subconscious states, racial distinctions, criminal and morbid types." Ghosts and witches were signs of superstition, not "personifications of conscience." Nor should Shakespeare be read as having any relevance to politics. The English history plays and the Roman plays "are political plays with the politics left out." Here was a gauntlet thrown down on behalf of historical correctness. "Ours is the day of the historical method," Stoll declared. "Fetichism [*sic*; what he called the "cult" of Shakespeare] is all that stands in the way."[19]

More recently, when Terry Eagleton's book on Shakespeare was published in 1986, reviewers zeroed in on what they called its "anachronisms." "Mr. Eagleton does in print what directors regularly do on stage," said the *New York Times*, "change the century, stitch up new costumes, but preserve the story-line and language." Herbert Mitgang found Eagleton "bold" and "courageous" but also sometimes "maddening." "Rather ingeniously, Mr. Eagleton united Freud and Marx in discussing *The Merchant of Venice*," he notes, although by 1986 this had become a fairly common starting point for discussions of the play. "Inevitably, Mr. Eagleton turns to Lady Macbeth to interpret militant feminists," he observes, adding that "it is doubtful if present-day women's organizations . . . would accept Lady Macbeth as a role model. The parallel is too narrow and strained." (Little did he know what a goldmine Hillary Clinton was going to be for Lady Macbeth hunters in the daily press. The comparison between these two politicians' wives became a standard trope of journalism in the 1990s.) When Eagleton alleges slyly that "Though conclusive evidence is hard to come by, it is difficult to read Shakespeare without feeling that he was almost certainly familiar with the writings of Hegel, Marx, Nietzsche, Freud, Wittgenstein and

Derrida," Mitgang regards this as more playful than persuasive. There seems to be something exciting about anachronism, then, and at the same time something illicit. What does this have to do with the relations between history and literature?

III

Let me offer an example of the seductiveness of history for me that also rang some alarm bells, reminding me of where my own resistances and textual predilections lay. A gifted young teacher of colonial American literature and culture recently explained a technique he had developed for teaching the seventeenth-century American poet Anne Bradstreet, whose work, he suspected, might seem temporally distant to his presentist young students. The poem he wanted to discuss was Bradstreet's "The Author to Her Book." Bradstreet wrote it after her brother-in-law, without her knowledge, brought a manuscript of her verses to London and had them published under the title *The Tenth Muse, Lately Sprung Up in America*. Here is the beginning of the poem, in which Bradstreet addresses her pirated book, describing it as the victim of a kidnapping:

> Thou ill-formed offspring of my feeble brain,
> Who after birth didst by my side remain,
> Till snatched from thence by friends, less wise than true,
> Who thee abroad, exposed to public view,
> Made thee in rags, halting to th' press to trudge,
> Where errors were not lessened (all may judge).
> At thy return my blushing was not small,
> My rambling brat (in print) should mother call,
> I cast thee by as one unfit for light,
> Thy visage was so irksome in my sight:
> Yet being mine own, at length affection would
> Thy blemishes amend, if so I could:
> I washed thy face, but more defects I saw,
> And rubbing off a spot still made a flaw,
> I stretched thy joints to make thee even feet,
> Yet still thou run'st more hobbling than is meet . . . . [20]

The poem is clearly imagined in the genre of the title, "the author to her book." The phrase "even feet" denotes "regular metrics," the "rags" suggest rag paper, and so forth.

My acquaintance, a scholar of puritan America, knowing the social and medical history of the period, and mindful of another poem by Bradstreet, "Before the Birth of One of Her Children," in which the poet anticipated the possibility of dying in childbirth, handed out to his students, as a way of making Bradstreet's words vivid and her historical predicament clear, photocopies of early-seventeenth-century articles and woodcuts of deformed children and monstrous births, a familiar preoccupation of recent early modern scholarship. When his students had sufficiently put themselves in the place of a mother contemplating anxieties attendant upon childbirth in a medically rudimentary context, he gave them another historical grid to defamiliarize their own sense of corporeal vulnerability. In puritan America, deformed children signified that the mother had consorted with the devil. Thus the fear and fascination was itself a sign of religious, not just medical, history. For this literary scholar—and here is my point—the cause or ground of interpretation was the historical situation: the historical fact and the historical framework through which it was viewed. Bradstreet's references to the "ill-formed offspring" were troped on a mother's hopes and fears.[21]

But Anne Bradstreet, who wrote in the mid-seventeenth century, was well read in sixteenth- and early-seventeenth-century English literature, including the works of Sir Walter Raleigh, William Camden, and Sir Philip Sidney, as well as Joshua Sylvester's Du Bartas's *Divine Weeks*.[22] Imagine if, instead of contemplating the fate of deformed children in the colonies, we were to juxtapose to her poem "The Author to Her Book" the following passage:

> It had been a thing, we confesse, worthie to haue bene wished, that the
> Author himselfe had liv'd to haue set forth, and ouerseen his owne writings;
> But since it hath bin ordain'd otherwise, and he by death departed from
> that right, we pray you do not envie his Friends, the office of their care,
> and paine, to haue collected & publish'd them; and so to have publish'd
> them, as where (before) you were abus'd with diuerse stolne, and surrepti-
> tious copies, maimed, and deformed by the frauds and stealthes of iniurious

impostors, that expos'd them: euen those, are now offer'd to your view cur'd, and perfect of their limbes; and all the rest, absolute in their numbers, as he conceived them.[23]

This is the letter "To the great Variety of Readers," Shakespeare's friends and fellow-players, John Heminge and Henry Condell, affixed to the First Folio of his plays. The similarities are so striking as to be obvious: the parent who was unable to oversee the publication of his writings, the (consequent) maiming and deformation of the text, the need in particular to regularize the meter (Bradstreet's "even feet," Heminge's and Condell's "absolute . . . numbers") and so on. It will not escape your attention that this text, too, is from the past—that is, embedded in the history of the period. It is not a late-twentieth-century product, juxtaposed to the seventeenth century. I would be quite willing to defend and indeed promote the use of anachronism for reading, but for now I want only to point out a difference between what might be called the vehicle and the tenor of historical literary scholarship. To illuminate Anne Bradstreet's poem "To Her Book" by framing it with images of "real" deformed children and information about death in childbirth is one kind of reading. To examine the same poem by considering it to be, itself, a legitimate or illegitimate offspring of a famous textual passage and a familiar figure of speech is another. The "Author" referred to in the First Folio's prefatory letter is also (like the speaker in Bradstreet's poem) said to have "conceived" his writings, which were "expos'd" by thieves just as Bradstreet's works were "snatched" and "exposed to public view."

Which is the "ground" here? Literary trope or social condition? Text or life? Figure of speech or historical fact? Every piece of writing inhabits these various worlds, and every text offers a dilemma, or an opportunity, in terms of its frames of reference. We have perhaps overcorrected earlier literary histories that confined texts within a world of other texts. But might not the intertextual references have shaped this poem as much as the medical realities? It seems that this question is all the more urgent in the case of a woman poet. Why are anxieties about reproduction seen as more real or more literal here than anxieties about authorship? Are women more naturally literal—less involved with literary history—than men? And could it be that in this case the desire to have a more complete picture of history impedes, rather

than brings out, the female poet in whose name it is often undertaken? It is not necessary to my argument for Bradstreet actually to be referring to, or remembering,
or even half-remembering, the Folio letter. If she were, we could perhaps allege that
her modest demurral was in fact a bold claim in disguise: Bradstreet as successor to
Shakespeare. But I do not care, at least right now, whether this is the (historical) case.
And I do not want, either, to dismiss or impugn the usefulness of historical context
and the power of contemporary images of childhood and deformity. This is not an
either/or issue. It is, instead, a question of the goals sought by a discipline, or the
practitioners of that discipline. Why do we read literature? Why do we teach it? What
do we teach?

IV

The defense of Shakespearean anachronism has a long and distinguished history. The
German romantic critic August Wilhelm Schlegel observes that Shakespeare "considered himself entitled to the greatest liberties. He had not to do with a petty hyper-
critical age like ours, which is always seeking in poetry for something else than poetry;
his audience entered the theatre, not to learn true chronology, geography, natural
history, but to witness a vivid exhibition. I undertake to prove that Shakespeare's
anachronisms are, for the most part, committed purposely, and after great consideration. It was frequently of importance to him to bring the subject exhibited, from
the back ground of time, quite near to us."[24] For Schlegel, Shakespeare's anachronistic mention of Hamlet's education at a university, "though in the age of the historical Hamlet there was not yet any university," was a sign of the playwright's wisdom
rather than of his ignorance: "He makes him study at Wittenberg, and no selection
could be more suitable. The name was very popular from the story of Dr. Faustus . . .
it was of particular celebrity in Protestant England, as Luther had taught and written there shortly before, and the very name must immediately have suggested the
idea of freedom in thinking." Concerning Richard III's mention of Machiavelli,
Schlegel "cannot even consider it an anachronism," since the word is used "alto-

gether proverbially." Anachronism, he insists, is an intelligent mode of generalization, as when early Christian painters dressed "the Saviour, the Virgin Mary, the Patriarchs and Apostles in an ideal dress," but the subordinate actors or spectators of the action in "the dresses of their own nation and age," or when an old manuscript shows the funeral procession of Hector, the coffin carried into a Gothic church. As with Shakespeare, so also with these artists: "a powerful consciousness of the universal prevalency and the solid consistency of their manner of being, an undoubted conviction that it has always so been and will continue so to be in the world" were crucial to the power of their work.

Perhaps anachronism—playing fast and loose with history—is not just something that sometimes happens to literature, but is connected to it in a more profound way. Suppose we return for a moment to Shakespeare's *Julius Caesar,* not by accident the locus classicus of some favorite literary anachronisms. That striking clock, for instance. Arden Shakespeare editor David Daniell reminds us, citing Sigurd Burckhardt's important essay on the topic, that the warring systems of the calendars were very much an issue of contention in late-sixteenth-century Europe, and that Julius Caesar had himself sorted out an earlier set of calendrical discrepancies. The Julian calendar, named in his honor, was the official calendar of Protestant England, while the "New Style" Gregorian calendar, named after the Pope, reigned throughout Catholic Europe. The striking clock, which, as Daniell notes, "amused and irritated eighteenth- and nineteenth-century commentators for its anachronistic ignorance,"[25] was in fact a powerful sign. Caesar had not only set the date with his reforms of the calendar, but also "set the clocks of Rome," and his commentaries are full of his concern for timekeeping. The clock and its striking are thus reminders within the play text of Caesar's power over and against Brutus's.

Julius Caesar contains a number of other celebrated anachronistic references, some of them sartorial: a reference to "hats," for example, describing the conspirators before the murder: "Their hats are pluck'd about their ears / And half their faces buried in their cloaks" (2.1.73). Alexander Pope found this so unhistorical that he printed the line "their—are pluckt about their ears"—"as if the word [hat] were some obscenity," observes Daniell, who adds, "Quite apart from the fine dramatic furtiveness of Shakespeare's image, the Romans did wear headgear," and sends the reader to the previous Arden edition, where we are told the particulars of that headgear: "the petasus, a broad-brimmed traveling hat or cap, the pilleus, a close-fitting, brimless hat or cap, worn at entertainments and festivals, and the cucullus, a cap or hood fastened to a garment." We also learn that Pope was "similarly unwilling to accept *hat*" in *Coriolanus,* where he emends the word to *cap* (*Cor.* 2.3.95, 164).[26]

The same criticism might be made of the reference to the turned-down "leaf" in Brutus's book (*JC* 4.3.271–72: "is not the leaf turned down / Where I left reading?"). Living in ancient Rome, Brutus would properly be reading from a scroll, not a codex, a book with leaves. The sleeping Imogen in another of Shakespeare's Roman plays, *Cymbeline,* also folds down the leaf of a book as she falls asleep (*Cymb.* 2.2.4). But of course by the time we get to *Cymbeline,* ancient Britain, Rome, modern Italy, and rural Wales are all nicely mingled in a transhistorical stew. This is not a mistake; it is a point.

Whether such temporal dissonances are admired or scorned, anachronisms in literature have their purposes and their effects. We see this very clearly and obviously as well in the history of performance, where the tension between so-called "modernization" and equally so-called "period costume" (also known as "museum Shakespeare") is the frequent target of theatrical reviews. Thus the director JoAnne Akalaitis, often criticized (or lauded) for the chances she takes with Shakespeare, is described in a review of her production of *Henry IV* (parts 1 and 2) as surprisingly conventional: "performed in predominantly period costumes . . . the production has only occasional anachronisms—a TV or telephone thrown in to drive home a motivation."[27] Peter Sellars has staged *Antony and Cleopatra* in a swimming pool and put King Lear in a "kingmobile" (aka a Lincoln Continental). The scheming villain Aaron in Julie Taymor's *Titus* (a film version of *Titus Andronicus,* set in ancient Rome) seals Titus's hand in a ziplock plastic bag.

Charles Spencer, assessing Michael Boyd's Royal Shakespeare Company production of *Troilus and Cressida* in 1998, began by declaring that he was "not one of those arch conservatives who believes that Shakespeare should always be staged in period costume," but went on to speculate about the setting: the scene opened with sepia photographs that seemed to evoke the western front during World War I, but many characters had Irish accents, and it eventually became clear that while the Trojans were Irish, the Greeks were British. "Why then," he wondered, "does Achilles look like a present-day Serbian war-crimes thug, and Ajax resemble a particularly dim heavy metal rock star?" Spencer admired the production, with reservations, and offered his own interpretation: "What Boyd is presumably trying to suggest is any modern, war-torn territory in which fine words cover vile actions."[28]

Some people love this kind of thing, and others hate it. Opinion was divided on the Baz Lurhmann film *Romeo and Juliet* with its black drag queen Mercutio and its CNN talking-head prologues. In Michael Almereyda's film *Hamlet* (2000), starring Ethan Hawke, letters are delivered by fax machine; Ophelia wears a wiretap to entrap Hamlet in the lobby scene; Rosencrantz and Guildenstern are heard on the speakerphone in Gertrude's bedroom; the prayer scene happens in a limousine, and Hamlet makes an indie video film of *The Mousetrap* to catch the conscience of the king. (Elsinore is a hotel. Denmark is a corporation. Claudius is a CEO. So runs the world away.) But these uses of anachronism, however startling, function by destabilizing juxtaposition: bringing a metaphor to devastatingly literal life, or striving, like the Boyd *Troilus,* for the postmodern version of timelessness—that is, multitimeliness. Some productions do this via costume, mingling classical dress, Nazi uniforms, 1970s punk- and 1930s gangster-wear. Others do it through cross-casting, mixing nations, races, genders, and accents.

Whether or not we like it, we have become accustomed to this mode of theatrical anachronism, as we have to its more moderate and "straight" avatars, modern dress and rehearsal clothes. Indeed even if we cherish the old ways, and hang an engraving of Mrs. Siddons as Lady Macbeth on the wall, we will have to acknowledge that she too is in "modern dress," and not in authentic "period costume"—whatever that would be: authentic Jacobean costume—or authentic medieval Scottish garb? As Eric Hobsbawn and others have argued about "the invention of tradition," authenticity is itself a cultural effect.

Using historical data anachronistically is different, of course, from the anachronistic use of theoretical ideas. But the reviewer who accused Terry Eagleton of anachronism seems himself to have conflicting notions of history and chronology as they affect literary interpretation. He subscribes to two inconsistent, but widely held, fantasies: the fantasy of historical determination, and the fantasy of universality. Thus he can say both that Eagleton's "strongest arguments are backed by history"—for example, the information "that inflation in the 1590s led to debased coinage and speculation" and also that political analysis of the plays is misguided: "Is not the range of [Shakespeare's] characters neither conservative nor even neoconservative but universal?"[29] I want here to contest both of these views—that history is data and that "universality" is something different from the theories it opposes, rather than being yet another theory.

There is a great deal that history can do for literary study, and for the study of Shakespeare and his contemporaries. I am not urging a return to the old days of timeless transcendence. The criterion for "timelessness" is the most historically time-bound thing of all, since there is no real evidence for it other than consensus. The timeless is what has stopped being considered a theory and has passed into stereotype. But there are some things history cannot do, and those things are, I want to insist, at the core of the literary enterprise.

V

I will illustrate this claim in my own anachronistic and unhistorical fashion by citing a well-known passage of literary criticism that addresses not a Renaissance text but a nineteenth-century one. The writer is discussing a particular kind of "research," the kind called a "search." (The two words search and research are version of the same.) Here he discusses a search of the premises undertaken by detectives:

> We are spared nothing concerning the procedures used in searching the area submitted to their investigation: from the division of that space into compartments from which the slightest bulk could not escape detection, to needles probing upholstery, and, in the impossibility of sounding wood with a tap, to a microscope exposing the waste of any drilling at the surface of its hollow, indeed the infinitesimal gaping of the slightest abyss. As the network tightens

to the point that, not satisfied with shaking the pages of books, the police take to counting them, do we not see space itself shed its leaves like a letter?

But the detectives have so immutable a notion of the real that they fail to notice that their search tends to transform it into its object. A trait by which they would be able to distinguish that object from all others.

This would no doubt be too much to ask them, not because of their lack of insight but rather because of ours. For their imbecility is neither of the individual nor of the corporative variety; its source is subjective. It is the realist's imbecility, which does not pause to observe that . . . what is hidden is never but what is missing from its place, as the call slip puts it when speaking of a volume lost in a library. And even if the book be on an adjacent shelf or in the next slot, it would be hidden there, however visibly it may appear. For it can literally be said that something is missing from its place only of what can change it: the symbolic. For the real, whatever upheaval we subject it to, is always in its place; it carries it glued to its heel, ignorant of what might exile it from it.[30]

The real is what the realist does not find. The belief that the real can be exhaustively measured and mapped is a form of blindness. The real is what escapes that mapping. The real is what literature, not "the world," is hiding.

The passage I have just quoted is taken from Jacques Lacan's reading of Edgar Allan Poe's "The Purloined Letter," and it is conceivable that Lacan's view of Poe may seem far removed from the study of either Shakespeare or history. So let me place next to this an uncannily similar passage from the works of Ralph Waldo Emerson's "Shakspeare; Or, The Poet." In that essay, published in the 1850 volume *Representative Men,* Emerson had this to say about "the researches of antiquaries, and the Shakspeare Society":

> [T]hey have left no book-stall unsearched, no chest in a garret unopened, no file of old yellow accounts to decompose in damp and worms, so keen was the hope to discover whether the boy Shakspeare poached or not, whether he held horses at the theatre door, whether he kept school, and why he left in his will only his second-best bed to Ann Hathaway, his wife . . . .
>
> The Shakspeare Society have inquired in all directions, advertised the missing facts, offered money for any information that will lead to proof; and with what result? . . . they have gleaned a few facts touching the property, and dealings in regard to property, of the poet. It appears that, from year to year, he owned a larger share in the Blackfriars' Theatre . . . that he bought an estate in his native village . . . that he lived in the best house in Stratford; was intrusted by his neighbors with their commissions in London,

as of borrowing money, and the like . . . . About the time when he was writing Macbeth, he sues Philip Rogers, in the borough-court of Stratford, for thirty-five shillings, ten pence, for corn delivered to him . . . . I admit the importance of this information. It was well worth the pains that have been taken to procure it.

For Emerson, "we are very clumsy writers of history." The questions we ask are the wrong questions, our real is the wrong real. Emerson feels so strongly about this that he claims to prefer knowing nothing of the specifically historical as it affects the case of Shakespeare, lest that knowledge impinge upon imagination and poetic genius:

> Can any biography shed light on the localities into which the *Midsummer Night's Dream* admits me? Did Shakspeare confide to any notary or parish recorder, sacristan, or surrogate, in Stratford, the genesis of that delicate creation? The forest of Arden, the noble air of Scone Castle, the moonlight of Portia's villa, "the antres vast and desarts idle" of Othello's captivity—where is the third cousin, or grand-nephew, the chancellor's file of accounts, or private letter, that has kept one word of those transcendent secrets?

Thus Emerson offers his famous and paradoxical assertions: that "Shakspeare is the only biographer of Shakspeare," and that "So far from Shakspeare's being the least known to us, he is the one person, in all modern history, known to us."[31] Not knowing Shakespeare's history is what gives Emerson his Shakespeare.

This rhetorically framed either/or choice, between the historical/archival and the imaginative/poetic ("Can any biography shed light on the localities into which the *Midsummer Night's Dream* admits me? . . . where is the third cousin . . . or private letter, that has kept one word of those transcendent secrets?") is just what has been debunked and analyzed in late-twentieth-century literary scholarship. To contemporary scholars there is no methodological contradiction, no doubt that historical research can and does illuminate imaginative writing, enriching rather than impoverishing aesthetic response.

Far from supplying a text's ground, historical study can unground it in a new way. Productions of *The Merchant of Venice* have been used both to inflame feelings of anti-Semitism and to critique them, depending upon the director's and actor's interpretation and ("always historicize") the culture and circumstances of production. Notice that the word *production* here has two equal and adjacent meanings. But as the example of *Merchant* suggests, once they are written, plays and poems and novels take on a life of their own, and even an "intention" or intentionality of their own—what is sometimes called the "unconscious" of the text. Their history starts with their writing and reading, is never completed, and can never been completely known.

It is worth remembering that the history of literary analysis has itself been dialectical. Thus in the course of the past century of literary study, philology and editing have given way to literary history; then to "character criticism" and psychology; then to close reading and the pursuit of images and themes; then to archetypal criticism; then to philosophical and psychoanalytic theory; then to historicism and an emphasis on socially and culturally produced categories like race, class, gender, and sexuality; and now once again to philology and editing (and "the history of the book") as well as to appreciation (also known as "aesthetics") and value (also known as "ethics"). The return of these last two categories, aesthetics and ethics, was in retrospect virtually guaranteed by their previous abjection, just as that abjection was virtually guaranteed by their enormous earlier success and prestige.

The critique of what is often called "presentism" by scholars of early modern literature and culture has been a necessary corrective for a failure of historical specificity that can obscure what is most striking and powerful about a literary text. The days of Jan Kott's frisky *Shakespeare Our Contemporary* have, to a certain extent, given way to the rigors, and longeurs, of Shakespeare Not Our Contemporary. But it seems equally crucial to acknowledge that some kinds of literary questions—questions about "what repeats"—cannot be posed through a predominantly historical approach.

Furthermore, there is yet another pertinent paradox for us to note: What the best literary historicists look for is not the moments when the author is consciously historical but when he or she is unconsciously historical. Anachronism or fantasy, which seems to escape historical determination, is intimately connected to it in ways that escape the author's conscious perception. Thus, in neglecting the ahistorical, literal-minded literary historicists are in reality neglecting the historical. And it is the analysis of the historicity of the present that prevents "presentism."

VI

"The injunction to practise intellectual honesty usually amounts to sabotage of thought," writes Theodor Adorno with characteristic acerbity. He continues:

> The writer is urged to show explicitly all the steps that have led him to his conclusion, so enabling every reader to follow the process through and, where possible—in the academic industry—to duplicate it. This demand not only invokes the liberal fiction of the universal communicability of each and every thought . . . but is also wrong in itself as a principle of representation. For the value of a thought is measured by its distance from the continuity of the familiar . . . . Texts which anxiously undertake to record every step without omission inevitably succumb to banality, and to a monotony related not only to the tension induced in the reader, but to their own substance.[32]

In Adorno's critique of demands for intellectual honesty, we can dimly make out what we are asking literature to do. Literature, in fact, is the discourse in which the knowledge of the discontinuity of thought is made fleetingly available. "The demand for intellectual honesty is itself dishonest," he writes, since it ignores or rejects the messier ways in which knowledge is actually acquired "through a network of prejudices, opinions, innervations, self-corrections, presuppositions and exaggerations." If "honest ideas" always manifest themselves as "mere repetition, whether of what was there before or of categorical forms," something crucial is missing in intellectual life. To illustrate this naiveté, he adduces an image of a man dying satisfied that his life has all added up. It is, as it happens, an image that carries a strong, though indirect, whiff of Shakespeare:

> Anyone who dies old and in the consciousness of seemingly blameless success, would secretly be the model schoolboy who reels off all life's stages without gaps or omissions, an invisible satchel on his back.

At first recollection, of course, Shakespeare's schoolboy in *As You Like It* is scarcely a model, that "whining schoolboy with his satchel / And shining morning face, creeping like snail / Unwillingly to school" (2.7.144–46). Why then associate this passage with Shakespeare at all? Why not think instead only of the modern German gymnasium student seemingly directly evoked by Adorno? There are two reasons: first, the indirect line of associative thinking is the one Adorno himself recommends in this passage ("a wavering, deviating line"; a kind of thought "which, for the sake of its relation to its object, forgoes the full transparency of its logical genesis"); second, the "mere repetition" of "categorical forms" is in fact present, in extreme form, in the passage where Shakespeare's schoolboy makes his appearance: Jaques' famous, or infamous, "Seven Ages of Man." It is Jaques who, to cite Adorno's phrase again, "reels off all life's stages without gaps or omissions, an invisible satchel on his back." It is Jaques, the "melancholy Jaques," who is the model schoolboy, showing off—here in parodic fashion—the well-worn "knowledge" which had by Shakespeare's time become a cliché:

> All the world's a stage,
> And all the men and women merely players.
> They have their exits and their entrances,
> And one man in his time plays many parts,
> His acts being seven ages. (2.7.138–42)

Instead of the diligent schoolboy, Adorno recommends the model of the slugabed and the truant:

> Every thought which is not idle . . . bears branded on it the impossibility of its full legitimation, as we know in dreams that there are mathematics lessons, missed for the sake of a blissful morning in bed, which can never be made up. Thought waits to be woken one day by the memory of what has been missed, and to be transformed into teaching.[33]

Teaching—like thought—depends upon what has been missed, upon the gaps in knowledge, the resistance to the idea of a citation of facts, a "discursive progression from stage to stage," the recording of every step without omission. It is in order to resist the inevitability of such a progression that I want to point toward the usefulness of anachronism, play, and all the other ways in which literature shocks us into awareness and preserves something that cannot be reduced to a ground. Whatever modes of reading are on the way, I hope that they and their practitioners will dare— at least from time to time—to be historically incorrect.

1   Claire McEachern, introduction to *Religion and Culture in Renaissance England,* ed. Claire McEachern and Debora Shuger (Cambridge: Cambridge University Press, 1997), 2.

2   Ibid.

3   Richard Bernstein, "We Happy Many, Playing Fast and Loose With History," *New York Times,* 18 January 2000, B1–B2.

4   Nabokov offers this piece of mindless and fictive "Ekwilist doctrine": "It is better for a man to have belonged to a politically incorrect organization than not to have belonged to any organization at all." Vladimir Nabokov, *Bend Sinister* (1947; reprint, New York: Vintage Books, 1990), 158.

5   Maurice Isserman recalls that among young people on the so-called New Left, the term was "always used in a tone mocking the pieties of our own insular political counterculture." Maurice Isserman, "Travels with Dinesh," *Tikkun* 6, no. 5 (1991): 82.

6   Ed Siegel, "Hazy Shade of 'Winter' at ART," *Boston Globe,* 19 May 2000, D1.

7   Clifford Longley, "Sacred and Profane: Labour and the Fall of Political Correctness," *Daily Telegraph,* 26 November 1999, 31. A recent publication by the British Institute of Economic Affairs, entitled "Political Correctness and Social Work," insisted that "anti-oppressive practice" was itself "oppressive as well as practically ineffectual." See "Social Workers Reject Political Correctness," *Times Home News,* 22 November 1999; Sue Clough, "Judge Attacks Irvine's Politically Correct Rules on Race," *Daily Telegraph,* 1 October 1999, 1.

8   Walter Benjamin, "Literary History and the Study of Literature," in *Selected Writings,* vol. 2 (1927–1934) (Cambridge, Mass.: Harvard University Press, 1999), 464.

9   See Samuel Kliger, *The Goths in England* (Cambridge, Mass.: Harvard University Press, 1952), cited in *Titus Andronicus,* ed. Jonathan Bate, Arden Shakespeare edition (Walton-on-Thames, Surrey: Thomas Nelson, 1997), 19–20.

10   Alan F. Segal, "The Ten Commandments"; Michael Grant, "Julius Caesar"; Carolly Erickson, "The Scarlet Empress," all in *Past Imperfect: History According to the Movies,* ed. Mark C. Carnes (New York: Henry Holt, 1995), 38, 44, 88.

11   Peter Desmond, "The Roman Theater of Cruelty," *Harvard Magazine,* September/October 2000, 22.

12   Michel de Montaigne, "Of Thumbs," in *The Complete Essays of Montaigne,* trans. Donald M. Frame (Stanford: Stanford University Press, 1958), 523:

> It was a sign of favor in Rome to close in and hold down the thumbs—
> *Your partisan with both his thumbs will praise your game.*
>
>   —Horace
>
> —and of disfavor to raise them and turn them outward:
> *When the people's thumb turns up.*
> *They kill their man to please them.*
>
>   —Juvenal

13   Philip Howard, "Blood and Circuses," *Times* (London), 17 May 2000, sec. 2, pp. 3–4.

14   Steve Allen, *Meeting of Minds* (Buffalo, N.Y.: Prometheus Books, 1989), 161, 82.

15   Don Freeman, "Scripts Made a Meeting of the Minds," *San Diego Union-Tribune,* 24 December 1989, entertainment section, 6.

16   Linda Nochlin, quoted in Sarah Boxer, "Snubbing Chronology as a Guiding Force in Art," *New York Times,* 2 September 2000, A19–A20.

17   Boxer, "Snubbing Chronology," A19–A21. Boxer cites British art critic David Sylvester in the *London Review of Books* and Jed Perl in the *New Republic.*

18   Iwana Blazwick, quoted in Boxer, "Snubbing Chronology," A21.

19   Elmer Edgar Stoll, "Anachronism in Shakespeare Criticism," *Modern Philology* 7 (1910): 1, 5, 7, 12, 8, 1, 19.

20   Anne Bradstreet, "The Author to Her Book," in *The Works of Anne Bradstreet,* ed. Jeannine Hensley (Cambridge, Mass.: Belknap Press of Harvard University Press, 1967), 221.

21   The editor of Bradstreet's works makes a similar claim: "In 'The Author to Her Book,' the metaphor of the book as a child expresses how the poet felt when she saw her work in print. It was her own child, even if she was ashamed of its errors." Jeannine Hensley, introduction to *The Works of Anne Bradstreet,* xxxi. The "new historicist" twist not found in this 1960s reading is the presentation of period images from authors like Ambroise Paré.

22   Adrienne Rich, "Anne Bradstreet and Her Poetry," in *The Works of Anne Bradstreet,* x.

23   John Heminge and Henrie Condell, "To the great Variety of Readers," prefatory letter, *The Norton Facsimile, The First Folio of Shakespeare,* prepared by Charlton Hinman (New York: W. W. Norton, 1968), 7.

24   August Wilhelm von Schlegel, "The Art of Shakespeare's Romantic Drama," from *Lectures on Dramatic Art and Literature,* trans. John Black (1808; London: George Bell and Sons, 1909), 356.

25   David Daniell, introduction to *Julius Caesar,* Arden Shakespeare, 3rd ser. (Walton-on-Thames, Surrey: Thomas Nelson, 1998), 17–22.

26   There is also in *Julius Caesar* the matter of "sleeves." "As they pass by, pluck Caska by the sleeve" Cassius instructs Brutus (1.2.178). "Togas had no sleeves," corrects John Dover Wilson in his Cambridge edition of the play. Once again the redoubtable Daniell comes to the rescue, suggesting that nearby references to cloak (1.2.214) and doublet (1.2.264) are clues that "Shakespeare also had London in mind," and reading the combination of pluck plus sleeve as, again, "almost furtive." These anachronistic references to clothing are, in other words, both functional and double-coded: their out-of-place-ness is a theatrical and interpretative marker, reminding the audience that the play is about now as well as then (Shakespeare's London as well as Caesar's Rome), while also drawing attention to a particular kind of affect (here "furtiveness").

27   David Patrick Stearns, "Akalaitis' Henry IV Conforms," *Gannet News Service,* 19 March 1991.

28   Charles Spencer, "The Arts: Shakespeare Meets Le Carre," *Daily Telegraph,* 9 November 1998, 19.

29   Herbert Mitgang, "Books of the Times," *New York Times,* 18 April 1986, C31.

30   Jacques Lacan, "Seminar on 'The Purloined Letter,'" trans. Jeffrey Mahlman, in *The Purloined Poe,* ed. John P. Muller and William J. Richardson (Baltimore: Johns Hopkins University Press, 1988), 39–40.

31   Ralph Waldo Emerson, "Shakspeare: Or, the Poet," in *Representative Men: Essays and Lectures* (New York: The Library of America, 1983), 716–21.

32   Theodor Adorno, "Gaps," in *Minima Moralia,* trans. E. F. N. Jephcott (London: Verso, 1978), 80.

33   Ibid., 81.

Lightning Source UK Ltd.
Milton Keynes UK
UKOW07f0836191115

263070UK00001B/13/P